D1551651

Muskrat

A Surprise Bid
For The America's Cup

by Douglas Hanks Jr.

I dedicate this book to Clayton and my father
who taught me the joy of sailing;
to Duck, Geezy and all my shipmates
whose company I have enjoyed,
and affectionately to
my lovely main sheet trimmer and wife, Xan,
for her limitless support and love

Any resemblance of the fictional characters to a real person is unintentional and coincidental. Certain real persons are mentioned in the book for purposes of adding reality to the story but obviously the fictionalized events involving either fictional characters or real persons did not occur.

Copyright © 1987 by Douglas Hanks, Jr.
TXU-270-198
The Library of Congress

All rights reserved, including the right of reproduction in whole or in part in any form.

First Printing, 1987
Second Printing, 1988
Third Printing, 1990
Fourth Printing, 1993

For information address
Muskrat
32 E. Dover St.
Easton, Maryland 21601

Glossary of Eastern Shore Terms

aland .... island
arster .... oyster
Balmer .... Baltimore
ca'm .... calm
drudge .... dredge
far .... fire
Gawd .... God
retare .... retire
tared .... tired
turkle .... turtle

Chapter One

Snow comes infrequently to the Eastern Shore of Maryland, especially before Christmas. A December storm, whether heavy or not, is a major event and is cause for serious celebration.

While most New Englanders slog grimly to and from work in near blizzard conditions, the tiny waterfront village of Oxford shuts down. Boatyards send employees home, shops close, and oyster tongers race back to their slips. As the first few flakes flutter down, it is as if an electric shock of excitement races through town. An early winter storm awakens within the people a sense of adventure and stirs imaginations that are normally as dormant as *mud turkles* in January.

Just such a storm crept in on December 20, 1985. The snow began in the early morning. Instinctively, Miss Lottie Dryden, at Dryden's Tavern, started icing down extra cases of "Budweiser™ longnecks" for the watermen who would surely be drifting in.

A few hearty oystermen hoping for some extra Christmas money had gone early to the nearest oyster bars. Most, however, had eyed the beginning flakes and, upon hearing that the snow was to continue all day, went back to bed. By mid-afternoon, all of them were engaged in serious business at another bar. They had gathered at Dryden's Tavern to drink Budweiser longnecks and exchange their favorite yarns. It would be these people who would set in motion events leading up to the now celebrated Eastern Shore challenge for the America's Cup.

Dryden's was jammed packed, and as the beer flowed faster, the room filled with cigarette smoke and the conversation became louder and louder.

"Had to use my compass today. First time since I got caught in the fog last spring eel pottin' on the Darchester shore."

"Shee-it, Eddie, you ain't got neither compass. If you had, you'd a got yourself over to Cap'n Neavitt Bozman's private arster bar and tonged on her while he couldn't see ya in the snow. "

"Ya don't need to do that, Eddie. This'd be a good day for you to go back and finish off the arsters that fella from Balmer City been plantin' under his wharf."

"I'll tell you one gawd damn thing, Eddie ain't gonna tong neither arster from under that fella's wharf again. He don't wanna read no more letters to the newspaper 'bout piratical watermen!"

Dryden's bar was small enough so that at any given moment a private conversation at one of the four tables could become general conversation. Often, the discussion at one table became so interesting that the people at the other tables fell quiet, except to offer a comment from time to time.

Dryden's sold more Budweiser longnecks than any other kind, but they also stocked other brands of beer for sissies and retirees. The retirees were a very nice group on the whole. They moved down from Baltimore or Washington and would buy an older Oxford home and redo it. As a result, the homes in town were steadily being restored. Every once in awhile, someone would move down from the city and "discover" Oxford, a town over three hundred years old. After living there for a few months, they'd stand up at a town meeting and enlighten the locals. "You all don't know what you've got. This is a great town we got here. You better be careful; a lot of people are gonna move down here from the city. We've got to be careful about that. We've got to be careful not to change anything." This made some people a little angry. But this type of retiree, fortunately, was the exception and not the rule.

Dryden's was more than a bar. They sold canned goods, potatoes and onions, and in season, Mrs. Dryden, known to the locals as Lottie, served oyster stew and crab cakes. It was a wonderful place to meet. After a hard day on the water, a cold beer and a hot cup of oyster stew hit the spot.

The tongers stayed on until a number of the evening regulars arrived. Gradually one conversation became dominant. People from the other parts of the room moved closer. They either became interested and dragged over a chair to join in, or stood listening for a few moments and shrugged into their coats made for the door, nodding to Lottie as they left. Lottie stood behind the counter and listened to their conversation as if she were hearing it for the first time. Actually, she had heard most of it many times before, since the main talker was her husband John, and the subject was one of his favorites. John Dryden liked to tell people who had only recently met him that he was a retired *former*. When they would express some wonderment at his career as a farmer, he would say, "Not farmer, former. Cap'n, I've been a former everything, almost. A crabber, trot-liner and crab potter, an arster tonger, hand and patent tonger, a pound netter and a market gunner. Never got caught once. I've been captain of a drudge boat, warrant officer in the Coast Guard, a wood butcher, house painter, pile driver, and now a store keeper. I don't intend to be a former store keeper though. I'm gonna be like my daddy and his daddy before him. Both of 'em come off the water and run this place 'til the day they died. No sir, I'm through being a former."

Although John was close to seventy, he looked as though he could still be any of the things he was formerly. Like many of the Eastern Shore's extraordinarily large men, he had the reputation of being gentle. His handshake was surprisingly soft. And though, like most of his fellow townsmen, he enjoyed a good argument, he would often defer to someone else's opinion when a discussion threatened to become ill-natured. Of course, everyone knew that John Dryden wasn't a man to be pushed too far. When pressed beyond his limit, he could become as violent as anyone else.

Tonight's discussion would not produce violence, however, but because it involved opinions about boats from men who had lived on or about the water all their lives, it was bound to be lively and argumentative. Talking with John Dryden were Hambden Martin and Hoyt Crane. Hambden's ancestors on both sides had made their living on the water where fishing, oystering, trapping, and shooting waterfowl were as much a part of the annual harvest as bringing in crops of tobacco in the old days, and grains and vegetables in the more recent past. Hambden himself had worked around boats since he was sixteen years old. His skills as a rigger, boat carpenter and marine engine mechanic had kept him employed in boatyards in hard and easy times. His innate feel for wind and water, and his unusual strength and agility had made him a much sought after crew member in ocean races and had gained him an occasional job as yacht captain. All of these qualities, along with the gift given to certain men to anticipate a wind shift or to seek out a private breeze, led him on to many a racing boat.

Now in his late thirties, Hoyt Crane was the youngest of the three men, yet he had spent almost as much time on the water as either of the others. He had been a pre-eminent racing skipper from the day he had first gotten his hand on the tiller of a Scrappy Cat at the age of seven. His capacity to make sailboats go fast, and his ability to get the best out of shipmates, had earned him berths on ten Bermuda races and a couple of Trans-Atlantic passages. He was truly a talented man when it came to a sailboat.

As the wind howled from the northeast and the snow came down harder, the conversation turned to sailing. It eventually led to the same topic it always did; the speed of skipjacks, the last commercial sailing vessels on the Chesapeake Bay and as oyster dredgers, the last working sail in the United States.

"They ain't neither yacht I've ever seen as fast as the *Maggie P*. Warn't nothin' could keep up with her."

John Dryden who had sailed or, as he would have said, "drudged arsters", aboard the *Maggie P*. told of the legendary speed of that particular member of the oyster fleet of fifty years ago. Hoyt Crane, as he often did, was voicing logical objections to what seemed to him purely fabricated claims about a boat that he had never seen.

John said, "But she did race against yachts. People have forgotten. Back in the thirties there was all sorts of boats in the Cedar Point Race. Mostly cruising yachts, of course, but sometimes even Star Boats went, and in 1936 the *Maggie P*. went, too."

"Wait just a gawd damn minute, John. Don't all them racing yachts have handicaps, time allowances just like log canoes have, so the little ones or the ones with less sail area or whatever, git more time to finish the race than the faster ones? Ain't neither drudge boat ever had no handicap."

Hambden Martin chose to answer the man who had raised this objection. "That's right. The *Maggie P*. didn't have no handicap, but all's she wanted to do was race boat for boat with the fastest yachts around. She warn't eligible for a trophy nohow. I was just a boy then. I cain't remember how she done."

"She done fine," John said. "In them days, the Cedar Point Race started off Gibson Island at the mouth of the Magothy River. There warn't no bridge then to worry 'bout. The race started 'bout noon the Saturday b'fore Labor Day. They usually finished up sometime Sunday mornin'. The course was the same as it is nowdays 'cept now they round the buoy that's further down the bay. Anyway, it's down to the mouth of the Patuxent and back, 'bout 80 miles all told."

Everybody leaned back with their Budweiser longnecks and listened to John Dryden as he told the story of the Cedar Point Race of '36. "Twarn't no different in '36 than it is now. Shee-it! The race was the easy part. The hard part was gittin' the boat to the starting line without runnin' aground or hittin' somethin', and keeping the skipper and crew away from fights and out of jail.

"Samuel E. Johnson III bought the *Maggie P.* in 1935. She was fifty-five feet long and for some unknown reason she was fast as a cut cat. Cap'n, when she had about fifteen to twenty knots and a cracked sheet, she'd go by everything on the river like they was tied.

"Now Sam was one of them rich fellers from New York. He come down here to retare and took up sailing. You all know Sam, whenever he'd lose a race he'd buy another boat. Shee-it! One time he had seven boats and neither trophy. Well, he finally realized that it weren't the boat's fault, it was his. So he called Hoyt Crane's father, Harry, and asked him to skipper his new boat, the *Maggie P....*"

John's story of the race went something like this:

In the summer of '36, Harry and his crew left Oxford before

6

Saturday's Cedar Point Race. It was Friday afternoon and there was a light southerly blowing up the bay. They had no engine and for fear of light air, brought no less than eleven cases of cold beer. Sam Johnson had a business meeting and couldn't make the trip over. He was to meet them early the next morning in Annapolis and then head for the starting line.

At 10:15 Friday night, the *Maggie P.* finally arrived in Annapolis. Everybody aboard was as drunk as a monkey, especially Harry Crane. The Yacht Club wouldn't let them tie up there, so they anchored out. One of the crew swam into the club and stole a dinghy and ashore they went. They hit every bar in town.

At about 2:30, the crew decided they had better get back to the boat. There was a race tomorrow and the skipper, Harry, had left an hour ago. They got down to the dinghy and after some very tricky manuevering, made it to the *Maggie P.* safely. Upon going below, they were surprised to find that Harry was not back. "Oh well, Harry must have found a honey—he'll be O.K.," and they went to bed.

At about three o'clock, Harry woke up. He had no earthly idea where he was. It was pitch black. He felt around and realized his pants were gone. He stood up from his sitting position and hit his head--hard. "Where in Christ's name am I," he said to himself.

He took a step and tripped. There was something tied around his ankles. It appeared as though someone had robbed him, taken his pants and tied him up. He crawled to a wall and found a knob. When he touched it, there was this terrible noise that sounded like an outboard motor and there was a rush of hot wind. In his panic, he found a wall switch and tripped the lights. He then realized that the noise was an electric hand dryer, the things around his ankles were his pants, and that he had passed out on the hopper in the Annapolis Yacht Club's men's room.

Harry pulled his pants up and stumbled out of the club. He was still as drunk as he could be. He wandered down to the dock, but found no dinghy. He could see it trailing astern of the *Maggie P.* At least his crew was aboard, but how in the hell he would get to the boat, he didn't know.

As he stood there in his drunken stupor, he heard a horse coming over the wooden Spa Creek Bridge. As the horse got closer, he could see that the rider was a city policeman obviously making his regular rounds. Harry ducked behind a tree. It would be hard to explain what Harry was doing on the yacht club grounds at 3:30 in the morning, especially since he was so drunk he couldn't talk.

The horse trotted by Harry, passing within ten feet, and continued up the street. Suddenly, the sound of the hooves stopped. Harry's heart was pounding. He knew the cop had spotted him. He peeked around the tree and saw the cop tie the horse to a post and head toward a house on the opposite side of the street. There was a light on in a second floor window. The cop went in and, within five minutes, the upstairs light was out.

Harry didn't budge for several minutes. Then he had an idea. "The horse! Horses can swim! That's how I'll get to the *Maggie P!* I'll steal the cop's horse!"

He stumbled down the street, untied the horse and off they went! What a sight that must have been: Harry on the cop's horse heading toward Spa Creek and the *Maggie P.*

Whether or not the cop heard them is unknown. He may have thought the head of the house had done the stealing.

Harry hung on for dear life, and when they came to the water, he somehow managed to coax the horse toward the boat. As they got close to the skipjack, Harry grabbed the dinghy, got in and climbed aboard the *Maggie P*. He still held the reins of the horse and he did what any good sailor does when leaving a dinghy; he made sure he securely tied the reins to a strong cleat before retiring for the night.

At around six-thirty, Harry was awakened by something pounding against the hull. He knew right away what it was; the cop's horse! He sprang out of his quarter berth and ran top side. The horse was drowning.

He untied the dinghy and tied the horse to it. He then headed for shore, towing the drowning animal behind. As they approached shore, an unexpected thing happened. When the horse felt the bottom, he took off like a shot for terra firma, and down Main Street he went in a full gallop, but this time he was doing the towing. Harry again was hanging on for dear life, being towed down Main Street in the dinghy by the cop's horse.

What a sight!

Harry was afraid to jump out. The street was brick and they were traveling so fast that planking started flying off the dinghy. To make matters worse, he spotted someone walking toward them reading a newspaper, completely unaware of what he was about to encounter. As they got closer, the man heard the deafening sound of the dinghy against the bricks and lowered his paper. Harry couldn't believe his own eyes. The gentleman behind the paper was none other than Samuel E. Johnson III heading for the *Maggie P*. He had arrived for the race.

As Harry and the horse passed by, Sam yelled in utter astonishment. "What in the hell are you doing, Harry?"

Soon Harry disappeared as they went around the bend heading for the town circle. As the horse entered the circle, a car appeared from nowhere. Before it could stop, it ran between the horse and the dinghy and cut the tow line in two, ending

Harry's unforgettable ride down Main Street.

The horse was never seen again, but probably is grazing far, far away from any navigable water.

The dinghy was completely torn up. The bottom was gone and what was left had taken a terrible beating. How Harry survived will never be known. He was not a pretty sight lying in the middle of the Town Circle amidst what was left of a stolen dinghy. Luckily, the cop was nowhere to be found. Harry picked himself up and headed for the club. There he found the *Maggie P.* approaching the dock and Samuel E. Johnson III pacing angrily.

As the *Maggie P.* came closer, Sam saw what seemed like several hundred empty beer cans, cigarette butts, and pieces of trash strewn from stem to stern. It looked like the crew had thrown a party for five hundred aboard. Harry walked down the dock and, with Samuel E. Johnson III, climbed on the skipjack. Sam didn't say one word. He just stood forward of the mast, his arms folded, surveying his disaster-stricken boat and six of the most hung-over crew members he had ever seen. Finally Sam walked back to the cockpit with fire in his eyes. "Harry, this God damn boat looks like shit! I paid a lot of money for this boat! I put you in charge, and you go off, get drunk, and trash my new boat!"

Harry's night had been a long one and he was in no mood for a lecture. He looked Sam in the eye and said, "Sam, count your blessings. She's still fifty-five feet long."

They headed up the bay toward the starting line. Everybody was in fair shape, except for Harry. He was on the leeward rail throwing up.

Samuel E. Johnson III was not pleased. He was looking forward to this race. He wanted to figure out what made the *Maggie P.* so fast. That's why he bought her. His plan was to find out what made her go and apply that knowledge to building a racing machine.

He had Harry Crane skippering the boat because Harry was the best. He hoped Harry might be able to figure out the secret, but he knew he couldn't do it on the leeward rail upchucking. A lot of races had been lost in the bar the night before the start, and Sam was afraid this was one of them.

The wind was still out of the south and had picked up to ten to twelve knots. They got to Baltimore light around eleven, in plenty of time for the twelve o'clock start.

Harry was feeling a little better and noticed the tide was flooding strong and would be a big factor in the start. Harry was known for his starts in the racing community. It was not uncommon for more than one boat to simply follow him at the ten minute gun. They figured Harry would win the start, and if they were on his tail they'd end up second best.

As the ten minute gun approached, Harry took the wheel. Sam had been steering. He liked to steer before the race so all the other people could see him, not realizing that Harry would actually have the helm during the race. Sam would make a point to pass close to all boats and speak to each one of them, wishing them good luck. He used to wear a white captain's hat, but Harry said if he continued to wear it he wouldn't go with him.

Harry timed the starting line three times. He ran it on starboard tack trying to find exactly how long it took to sail from the committee boat to the pin. The wind had some east in it and the line was set for due south air. The pin would be favored, but Harry wanted to be on starboard tack at the gun.

He'd run the line and hit the pin at the gun on starboard tack. That would prevent boats from simply starting on that end on port. Everyone knew that Harry would cut a port tacker in half if he tried to cross him.

The ten minute gun fired. That was Sam Johnson's signal to get real nervous. As soon as Sam heard a gun, he'd do strange things. He would check the depth sounder and bark out the water depth to Harry.

Harry would say, "Shee-it, Sam. We're in the middle of the damn'd bay. The gawd damn *Queen Mary* sails right through here. There's plenty of water."

Sam never listened to anybody between the ten minute gun and the start. When the five minute gun would fire, he'd get worse. That's when he would start repeating what Harry would say. For instance, if Harry said, "Ready about," Sam would yell at the top of his lungs, "Ready about--Everybody! We are tacking--Get Ready!"

As it got closer to the actual starting gun, he would get louder and start to cuss a lot. "Harry there's a God damn boat coming at us! Jesus, we are in forty feet of water! Shit, Harry...!"

Sometimes, he couldn't think of anything to say, so he'd just repeat something. One time he said, "Shit, Harry! Shit, Harry! Shit, Harry!" for a good thirty seconds.

Finally, Harry looked at him and said, "Sam, if I go now, you'll have to start this boat, so why don't you just sit down and shut up."

The five minute gun fired and Harry noticed a slight wind shift to the South. The pin was still favored, but not by as much. Most of the fleet were at the pin, positioning themselves for a port tack start. It took Harry one minute and ten seconds to run the line. At one minute and thirty seconds, Harry yelled, "Trim for speed!" They were heading for the line on a close reach and the *Maggie P.* had a bone in her teeth.

"Time!" Harry yelled, indicating he wanted to know how many seconds to the gun.

Sam yelled back, "One minute fifty-five seconds!" Sam was excited and added a minute. Harry knew what he did and didn't say anything. He did wonder how Sam was smart enough to make all that money, but couldn't keep his cool on a boat enough to read a stopwatch.

Harry noticed that the jib was all of a sudden calling for a huge ease. That meant the wind had hauled. "Ready about!" Harry yelled.

This was too much for Sam. He yelled, "Ready about, we're tacking. God damn it, there's a boat, Harry! God damn, we're in fifty feet of water! Shee-it, Harry!" By the time Sam was through, the boat was on a port tack heading back to the committee boat. Because of a stream of starboard tackers, Harry kept the boat up and went to weather of the Committee by two boat lengths and jibed. Just to leeward was *Avalanche*, a huge 70 foot yawl, yelling at Harry to "Keep up!"

"Time!" Harry yelled.

There were fifteen seconds to the gun and Harry seemed to be trapped. He was heading right at the Committee boat, a fifty-five foot Burger, and *Avalanche* was two feet to leeward. Both boats were moving very fast and Harry was having trouble keeping the *Maggie P.* up, away from the *Avalanche* who had the right of way.

Harry luffed up a little, but was within three boat lengths of hitting the Burger broadside. Some of the boys on the *Maggie P.* started getting concerned. Jack Bart was a crackerjack crew. He yelled to Harry, "You're going to have to tack Harry." Harry didn't budge. "We're going to hit the Burger."

Harry held his course. With ten seconds to the gun, Harry yelled to the skipper of *Avalanche*, "Keep your gawd damned boat down from a quarter luff or I'll toss your ass out right now! Keep it down!"

Avalanche came down a hair and the *Maggie P.* slid by the Burger with no more than a foot to spare.

Harry had won the start. Only he and *Avalanche* were on the right end of the line. When Harry was reaching for the pin end, the jib called for a big ease because the wind had shifted to the southwest. Harry knew at that moment that he had to change his tactics. As a result, the *Maggie P.* crossed the rest of the fleet by three boat lengths. When things had settled down, Jack Bart came aft and said to Harry, "I thought that you'd forgotten that Burger was fifty-five feet long."

Harry, concentrating on his sails said , "No, Jack, you had forgotten about the tide."

Harry had remembered that there was a strong flood tide shoving everyone up the bay away from the line, and that was what had provided the *Maggie P.* room at the gun.

"I guess I had forgot about the tide, but let me ask you somethin' else Cap'n Harry. What was that rule you was yelling at the *Avalanche* ?"

Harry just smiled, and after seeing that smile, Jack knew. There was no rule, but *Avalanche* didn't know it. "Those boys will probably wear out the rule book looking for that one," he thought to himself.

Samuel E. Johnson III was so excited about the start, he started slapping Harry on the back. "Great start, Harry! Great start! You did it boy! Great start!" With that, Harry leaned over the binnacle and threw up on him.

"Thanks, Sam," he said.

Sam was so mad that he went below to change his shoes and didn't come up until supper. The crew could finally get the details from Harry about what was banging against the hull that morning.

When Sam came from below around seven, the *Maggie P.*

was second. *Avalanche* had gotten ahead of her and had a sizable lead. The wind had gone back a little toward the south.

Sam had settled down and asked Harry about what the weather was going to do. Harry said it would go back to southwest and eventually go west and northwest. The tide had changed and was ebbing. Harry was in the ship's channel in the tide's strength.

"The place to be before too long will be on the western shore boys," Harry said. "I hope it doesn't go sou-west before dark."

"Well if that's the place to be, Harry, why don't we go over there now?" Sam asked.

"Shee-it, Sam, we can't go west 'til dark. Why in hell's name would we give them Annapolis boys a sailin' lesson? If we tacked now, half the damned fleet would go with us. Besides, we're in right smart tide out here."

So Harry stayed out in the middle and waited for nightfall. *Avalanche* stayed with the *Maggie P.* in the channel.

Jack Bart went below and fixed some soft crabs for dinner. He came up with soft crabs, fresh deep red sliced tomatoes, and some golden yellow sweet corn covered with salt, pepper and lots of butter. The crew needed a good meal, especially Harry. It was going to be a long night.

Later that day, as the sun disappeared, the *Maggie P.* was on starboard tack with the wind out of the south at less than ten knots. Harry was still driving, but tiring quickly. He asked Jack to get him two flashlights and some tape. He also directed him to find a piece of cellophane he had stowed below. Even though Jack didn't understand, he did what he was told.

Upon his return, Harry asked him to take the helm and told the crew to get ready to tack. Harry wrapped the red cellophane over one flashlight and taped it to the starboard side, aft of the wheel. He taped the other clear one forward on the bow

15

sprit. He placed a piece of tape over one half of the lens.

"Let's go right, boys." Harry said, "We've got to get to the western shore before the wind shifts. Ready about!"

Harry reached below and turned off the running lights. Sam yelled, "The God damned running lights went out, Harry! God damn! We'll be run over by a ship! We're all gonna die." Harry had turned them off, but would explain later.

Jack tacked the boat and Harry turned on both flashlights. "Now Sam, those Annapolis boys won't know what in Christ's name is happening. It'll look like we're goin' backwards on starboard tack to them while we're goin' west on port. Gotta keep 'em guessin', Sam. Gotta keep'em guessin'."

Harry went straight to the western shore. He wanted to get there before the change of tide and before the wind hauled west.

Avalanche couldn't detect the move. There were no lights that she could see. The boys behind could only see the red light aft and white forward, the same as they saw before the tack.

Harry told Jack not to pinch. "If you'll let her off a bit, our lights will look better to them boys behind. Better angle and all."

Only one boat saw the move and tacked to the west with them. It was a class A sixty footer called *Blue Streak.* She was about six boat lengths to leeward of the *Maggie P.*

As they sailed toward the west, the wind went light and the tide started to flood. Before too long, the tide was stronger than the wind and Harry noticed they were being taken up the bay.

"Listen boys, the tide's takin' us away from the mark. We gotta git our anchor over till this wind comes in. *Blue Streak* is right abeam and I don't want her to know what we're doin'. Jack, you quietly slip that anchor over the weather side. Now, when it's over, everybody's got to pretend we're still sailin' the boat. That way they won't anchor and we might gain some ground."

Jack slipped the anchor over and it held. Even though the *Maggie P.* was at anchor, Harry barked orders.

"Ease that jib a hair. That's it. We were over-trimmed. She's goin' good now."

He made sure his voice could be heard aboard *Blue Streak* as he added some more lies. "Wind's pickin' up a little. Trim the jib." Then he'd reach up and spin a winch.

Blue Streak's running lights began to fade as she was being set up the bay. Harry pulled a little tape off the flashlight lens so it would appear just as bright to the other boat. Before too long, the *Blue Streak* was out of sight.

Harry's trick had worked. The air came back and the *Maggie P.* hoisted her anchor and continued heading to the west. Harry went below for a little shuteye.

They reached the western shore around ten-thirty. Harry was asleep. The trick had seemed to work. No one followed except *Blue Streak*, and they had outsmarted her.

They were very close to shore when Jim Bob went below to get Harry. "We're close to running aground, Harry. We've got to tack. Is that O.K.?"

Harry, half awake said, "Jim Bob, I ain't never heard of anybody winnin' this race by running aground. Tack, fool! But don't go out too far. Go to twenty-five feet of water and then come back. And Jim Bob, better turn them running lights on again and kill them flashlights. Get me up around midnight."

They worked the shore and a little after eleven o'clock the wind went to the southwest on the change of tide. Harry was right again. For the moment, they were in great shape.

At midnight, Jim Bob woke Harry up. The Cedar Point turning flasher was in sight. Dave had done a good job. He was

17

good in the light stuff. He had kept her going and stayed out of the foul tide.

Harry felt good about the race so far. He felt they were in a good position. The wind had hauled more west, which meant a nice reach coming back up the bay in addition to a fair tide .

Just then they discovered some bad news. They saw *Avalanche* heading back up the bay under a full head of steam. She was under a spinnaker. Somehow she had stayed ahead in spite of the wind shift. Of course she was seventy-five feet long.

As they approached the flasher, they felt a little better. They were afraid more boats had made out and were ahead of them, but they saw no one. They were second in fleet, boat for boat, in a skipjack no less.

Harry thought to himself, "There really is something mysterious about the *Maggie P.* She shouldn't be this fast." He had to find out what it was. How this boat could be doing this well he didn't know. There was something about the *Maggie P.* that was a design breakthrough. What the hell was it? For whoever figured it out, it could mean millions of dollars.

At twelve fifty-three, the *Maggie P.* rounded the mark. They were almost twenty minutes behind *Avalanche*. Harry thought about what he could do to catch her. The wind was still southwest and building. "It should haul more west," he thought. She was moving well. She liked to be off the wind.

It was after one o'clock when Jim Bob Williams decided to get some shuteye. It didn't really matter. Harry had plenty of help, and Jim Bob wasn't a very good sailor anyway.

Harry once described Jim Bob to a friend, "I think he sailed so he could dress up. Jim Bob loved to dress up. He had the damnedest sailing clothes you ever saw. He'd arrive on the boat before a race with his pressed red pants on and snap shackles and a big knife dangling from his belt. I don't know what the snap shackles were for, but he used the big knife to cut the cheese after the race.

"Even though his feet smelled bad, he didn't wear socks because he didn't think that looked good. Jim Bob should have tried socks. He was always tripping and falling down on somebody. He'd usually fall during a jibe or a tack.

"He must have had trouble picking out shirts cause he'd always wear more than one. I remember one day he wore three shirts and it was ninety-five degrees out. I thought he'd die. He had the damnedest gloves you ever saw. They couldn't keep you warm. They had neither finger holes into 'em. Anyway he liked them gloves. He wore a hat kind of like Harry's. Harry's was khaki and had a brim. Just over the brim was a black patch with a gold sailfish jumpin'. Jim Bob's was like that 'cept his was dark blue and instead of the sailfish, he had a little round pin, like girls wear, and on it was a little tiny flag. He said it meant he was a member of some sailing club. I don't know how he got in. Shee-it. Jim Bob knew about as much about sailing as Harry did about camel racin'.

"Jim Bob's watch was funny too. It was real big and had five or six buttons to it. He said that while we were starting he could tell how much time was left by the color his watch turned. Anyway, Jim Bob was alright. He was a friend of Sam. That's how he got aboard. He was good company. That is except when it blew up. He didn't like rough weather at all."

As Jim Bob was falling asleep, he could hear thunder in the distance. He thought to himself, "I hope we're not getting a squall tonight."

It was a beautiful sail that night. The moon was full and the sky clear except for a couple of thunderheads off to the northwest. The wind went to the west and picked up, blowing about twenty to twenty-five knots. The *Maggie P.* was screaming up the bay. Now and then, they'd pass a racer heading for the turning mark. They had a good lead on the rest of the fleet.

After a bit, Harry asked Sam to take a trick at the wheel. That was unusual, but Harry was very tired and steering was fairly easy under the conditions.

Harry went below and got a beer. He noticed Jim Bob was tossing and turning in his bunk. He could tell by the shackles clinking and clanging. He came up and sat in the cockpit next to Sam. Dave and Nick Benson were sitting across from them.

Nick was twenty and worked at his father's boatyard in Cemetery Cove in Oxford. That's where the *Maggie P.* was built. Nick's dad, Ralph Benson, was a master builder. He had built some of the finest yachts ever to hit the water. Nick wanted to learn the trade and eventually take over when his dad retired.

When he wasn't sailing or working, Nick loved to whittle. He made a wooden chain twenty feet long one time. He also loved the *Maggie P.* He spent a lot of hours helping to build her and he was very proud to have played a part in her construction.

"She's walking up the bay, Sam." Harry said.

"Harry, this boat is fast as hell and I don't know why. I wish I did. She's got good sails, but that's not the answer. Her bottom is as smooth as an eel's ass, but that's not it either. It's hard to believe that a skipjack can go like this one. The *Maggie P.* is magic. She's got a secret Harry. We all know that. How can we figure it out?"

"Nick's father knows something nobody else does." Harry said, "Nick, what did your dad do to this boat?"

"My mother drowned all her dumb children, Cap'n Harry. If I told you in one minute what it's taken me ten years to learn, I'd consider my ten years a waste 'cept for one minute. I ain't sayin' I know all Dad's secrets, but I know a few. Dad can build a boat that's faster than anybody else's, I can tell you that."

Sam thought to himself, "I'll find out what Ralph Benson's secret is if it's the last thing I do and if it takes the last penny I have."

Harry was beside himself. He too felt compelled to find Ralph Benson's secret.

When they were abeam of Poplar Island, it got real dark to the north, and thunder and lightning were everywhere.

"Let me have the wheel, Sam. You better help Jack tuck in a reef. I think we're going to get a blow."

Nick gave a hand with the reef. The storm was very close and visibility ready to close in. Harry got a good compass reading and quickly put on his gear. It was raining hard just ahead and the wind was really kicking up. White caps could be seen not far to weather.

"Better tuck a reef in that jib while yo're at it, boys. This looks like a mean one!" Harry said.

Sam went below and got everyone's foul weather gear.

The second the reefs were in and foul weather gear on, it hit. There was no wind gauge aboard, but it must have gusted to fifty knots. The *Maggie P.* took one gust and put her jib boom in the water. It was blowing out of the northwest. Harry was on port tack and held it.

"Stay on that main, Dave. I'll need an ease when them white gusts hit!"

They were pretty far west when the squall hit, so they could hold port tack for a good while.

"Ease the main Dave!" The *Maggie P.* took a hard knock down. Harry was fighting the wheel trying to hold her down. Visibility was zero. The rain felt like little pins when it hit their faces.

"A little trim on the main." The *Maggie P.* was doing okay in spite of the terrible conditions.

"Where the hell is Jim Bob? He ain't overboard is he?" asked Sam.

"He's below, Sam. Better go get him and see if he's alright."

Jim Bob was sound asleep when Sam found him. He turned on a reading light over Jim Bob's head and discovered the greenest face he'd ever seen. Jim Bob was as sick as a dog.

"Better get topside, Jim Bob. The fresh air will make you feel better."

Jim Bob sat up and started putting on his gear. The cabin was in a shambles. Drawers had popped open and debris was everywhere.

Jim Bob felt awful. He had just gotten his foul weather pants on when a gust hit and the *Maggie P.* broached. From a galley shelf, on the weather side of the boat, flew a jar of mayonnaise. It hit the gimbaled table in front of Jim Bob, flew open and a huge glob of mayonnaise hit him in the face. Jim Bob raced for the companionway. What a sight it was; Jim Bob's green face smeared with white mayonnaise. He had mayonaise from the brim of his sailing club hat to his sockless feet, as he went to the leeward rail.

"Jim Bob! Don't get your ass overboard. They ain't passed that rule yet about finishing with all the crew."

Harry talked a big game, but everyone knew his crew's safety was important to him.

Nick went to leeward to give Jim Bob a hand. "I can't have two people to leeward in this squall." said Harry, "Git Jim Bob a bucket and both of you get to weather."

Nick and Jim Bob sat on the weather side of the cockpit. Nick was forward of Harry and Jim Bob forward of Nick with a bucket in front of him. Nick wasn't actively sick but after watching Jim Bob he felt a little queasy. His feet had gotten soaked when he went to leeward and were freezing.

"Jack, I figure we should be getting close to Bloody Point. Can you see anything? I'm thinking about tacking."

Jack looked around and asked Lenny to look to leeward. It was still raining cats and dogs and the wind was holding steady at thirty to thirty-five knots.

"I think I see something at one o'clock." Lenny spotted something, but wasn't sure what it was. "Better take a look, Harry, it's pretty close!"

Harry got to leeward of the wheel and took a look. "Ready about! Ready about! Let the jib go. Grab your bucket Jim Bob." He rolled the wheel and brought the *Maggie P.* about.

Dead to weather, only a boat length away, was *Avalanche*. They had caught her in the squall and damned near ran into her. Now they both were on starboard tack. They were so close you could hear what they were saying.

"It's that Gawd damn Eastern Shore skipjack. If they beat us boat for boat we won't be able to show our faces at the club for a year. I'm going to cover those bastards like a wet blanket. Let me know if it looks like they're going to tack."

Harry and the crew heard what was said. They were to leeward. The *Avalanche* crew couldn't hear them because of the high winds.

Harry had a plan.

"Let's false tack 'em boys. When I say so, everybody get up like we're going to tack. We'll go through the motions. I'll luff her up and you ease the sheets about three feet. I'll bring her back down and stay on this tack while the *Avalanche* goes. Ready?"

Harry yelled to the top of his voice. "Ready about!" The crew got up and went to their positions.

There was a lot of stirring on *Avalanche*. They were getting ready to cover. It looked like the trick would work.

"Hard-a-lee!" Harry yelled. Both sails were eased four feet as Harry brought her into the wind, then quickly fell off and continued his original course.

It didn't work. *Avalanche* didn't bite. They were going to, but someone at the last minute said to go back. So much for that. If it didn't work then, it won't now. They'll be ready next time.

They were getting close to the western shore. The crew of *Avalanche* never took their eyes off Harry and the *Maggie P*. The storm hadn't let up one bit.

"How the hell can we shake those boys," Harry thought to himself. Then it came to him. He chuckled to himself and smiled.

"What are you up to, Harry?" asked Jack.

"You'll see. But you can kiss *Avalanche's* little ass goodbye. Sam, when I tell you to, go up to the spar and point up the mast. Jack, can you find Thomas Point?"

"No, I don't see it, Harry."

"Tell me when you see our wake getting bigger, Jack!"

They headed for the western shore. When the *Maggie P*. began to foot on *Avalanche*, Harry had the mainsail eased to slow her down. Now the crew was really confused.

"What the hell are you doing, Harry? How in the name of hell are we going to beat *Avalanche* boat for boat by slowing down? Shit!" Sam was getting nervous again.

"Just hang on, Sam. We'll be alright."

"Harry, it looks like our wake's getting bigger."

"Sam, go forward and point up the spar." Sam had no idea what the hell was going on.

"Nick, get ready to pull the board up."

"They're aground, Harry! They hit! *Avalanche* is aground!" Sam yelled.

"No shit, Sam. I knew they was gonna run aground some time ago. She draws eight feet. They was watching you and looking up at our spar. Ain't no depth sounders up there. Gotta keep'em guessin', Sam. Gotta keep'em guessin'."

"Nick, pull up the board and let's go about." Harry tacked the boat and left the *Avalanche* hard aground in the middle of a squall. As Capt'n Harry predicted, they kissed their little asses goodbye.

"I still don't understand why you slowed the boat down Harry." Sam asked.

"*Avalanche* wanted to cover. You can't cover a boat that's ahead. We had set the trap and I wasn't going to let 'em out of it."

They had out smarted the *Avalanche* and were heading for the barn.

"How you feeling Jim Bob?" asked Harry.

"I'll be glad when this lets up a little bit. I can tell you that."

" How about you Nick?"

"I'm feeling better Cap'n Harry. My feet ain't as cold." It took him a little while to realize that Jim Bob had been throwing up in his boots, and that's why his feet were warming up. When he figured it out, he took over Jim Bob's bucket.

The squall finally let up at Sandy Point and the *Maggie P.* finished at six-fifteen Sunday morning. They didn't have a rating for the race, so no gun was fired. Nobody really cared. They had sailed a great race on a great boat. The wind was still northwest with some punch. They jibed around the committee boat and headed the *Maggie P.* for home.

Harry was exhausted. He went below for some well deserved rest. "Thank Christ we're not going to Annapolis." he

25

thought. "I wonder if that cop ever found his horse."

As they passed abeam of the Severn River, Harry was just dozing off when he heard Jack say, "Christ! There's *Avalanche* under power heading up the river. They must've used their engine to git off. Guess they ain't goin' to the club!" Harry went into a sound sleep.

Now that's John Dryden's story of the *Maggie P.* in the 1936 Cedar Point Race. Nobody could touch her."

The boys looked outside and it was snowing harder than ever. They were calling for the snow to continue through the night. There would be no markets tomorrow for sure. No way of getting the oysters to the city.

"What made the *Maggie P.* so fast, John? What was the secret?"

"There's only one person who knows, Hambden. Only one person. He was on that Cedar Point race. Nick Benson knows."

Nick's dad died in 1964. Nick was fifty-six when he had taken over the yard. Now his son John Allen was running it, but Nick, who was now seventy-eight, spent a lot of time there. When one of the men would try to cut a corner, like only put screws every foot instead of six inches, he'd raise hell and have them do it right. No corners were cut while he was around. More important, Nick knew the secret. Maybe John Allen knew too, but no one was sure.

"Did Sam Johnson ever figure it out?"

"No, Sam never did as far as I know. He had Ralph build him a racing boat in 1939. She was quick. When Ralph had her trimmed right, she would walk by the fleet, especially off the wind. Problem was, Sam didn't let Harry sail her. At any rate, the boat never did do that well, and finally Sam bought a power boat. He still talks about how fast Ralph's boats are though."

"Were Ralph's boats the fastest ever built?" Hambden

asked.

"I don't know, Hambden. I guess that boat from down under is the fastest one around now," said John. "That one that took the America's Cup to Australia. I seen pictures of her. She had a keel to her looked like she'd run up on a rock and split in two. It was flat like. When I seen it for the first time, the bottom of the keel lookin' forward looked like a kingfisher's wings 'tween beats. Never seen a keel like that 'fore. She beat all them fancy boats, like the *Courageous, Liberty,* and all. That's the worst gawd damn thing I ever seen, them takin' that cup from us. I'd sooner somebody shot my dog."

Drake Cochran had finished playing pool with Loscomb Willey, and they had both pulled up a chair. Drake joined in the conversation, "Yeah, they call them boats twelve seaters. Hold twelve people I guess."

"Gawd damn it, Drake, they ain't twelve seaters. They're twelve meters."

"Horse shit, John! How in Christ could they be twelve meters? If they're twelve meters, my gawd damn skiff is longer than Morris Street."

"Drake, that ain't how long it is, that's something 'bout the building rules. I ain't sure how it works. I'll bet Nick Benson could tell you."

Hoyt Crane got a little excited, pounding his ten-ounce on the table, and said in a very determined voice. "I'll bet you Nick Benson could build one of them suckers and beat the pants off that Australia boat."

"I'll bet yo're right, Nick. If he could build a skipjack that could stay with the *Avalanche*, he can sure as shit build a fast twelve."

"Wouldn't that be something? A twelve meter from Oxford gettin' the America's Cup back. Son-of-a-bitch!" Hambden

Martin was excited too.

John Dryden spoke up, "Nick Benson could build her up to Cemetery Cove and Hoyt Crane here is the best gawd damn skipper around. He could git up a good crew among the local boys. Why couldn't we go git that cup? She'd look right smart behind the bar there."

"Be good for business having that cup there John," added Lottie.

"Only one problem boys." John was losing his enthusiasm. With a rather blank expression, he looked down at the table and tapped his empty beer bottle a couple of times. "Who's going to pay for all this? You're talkin' lots of dough. Shee-it! You could trot line and tong 'til there wasn't neither crab or arster in the Tred Avon and couldn't pay for it. Them boats is expensive."

The room got real quiet. Drake Cochran broke the silence, "Shee-it. After you build the gawd damn thing you got to git it to Austria; wherever the hell that is. There's another right smart haul of oysters and crabs right there."

One of the boys corrected Drake, "It ain't Austria, Drake, it's Australia. That's the big island on the other side of the world. That's where all them kangaroos live."

Hoyt Crane started pounding his longneck on the table again. "I know! I know who would pay for it; Samuel E. Johnson III."

"Gawd damn, Hoyt, you're right, I'll bet Sam just might do it, especially if Nick Benson would build her and you'd agree to skipper."

Samuel E. Johnson, III was in his eighties, but was still in pretty good health and had retained his love of yachting. He lived up the Tred Avon on a lovely old estate. He still had a power boat—a beautiful fifty-five foot Trumpy. He had a captain who skippered her most of the time, but Sam could still handle her.

The excitement grew and pretty soon everybody's spirits were high. They were all pounding their longneck Budweisers on the tables, talking about the new twelve, who would crew, and their trip to Australia. It was decided that Hoyt Crane and John Dryden would go see Nick Benson in the morning, and if Nick agreed, they would pay a visit to Samuel E. Johnson, III.

"What are we goin' to name the boat, boys?"

"Gawd damn, Hoyt. We ain't even talked to Nick or Sam Johnson and you want to name her. Ain't that rushin' things a might?"

"Maybe so, John. But it don't hurt nothin'. Seems like a lot of them twelve meters have real patriotic names. There's *American Eagle*, there's *Liberty, Freedom* and there's the *Spirit of America, Stars and Stripes*. Names like that."

"There ain't nothin' that says it's got to be a patriotic name. We can name it anythin' we want," Hoyt said.

"I guess you're right. We could name it *Dryden's Bar, Cold Beer and Fifty Cent Crab Cakes from Oxford Maryland* if we want to."

The boys chuckled, "We ought to name her after something Eastern Shoreish though since she's built here and all. What could we name her?" asked John.

Drake had an idea. "We could call her *Piss Clam*."

"Gawd damn it, Drake, people would think you was bein' dirty. Hell, people on the other side of the bridge never heard of a piss clam, let alone the other side of the world."

"Guess your right, Hambden. Never thought of it like that."

"My daddy named his boat the *Eel*. Always thought that was right catchy. You know, how they slip through the water and all."

Hoyt had a thought. "*Canvasback* ain't a bad name for a boat. 'Specially with the canvas a twelve carries."

"That's a right good one, Hoyt. Not bad at all."

"Course, my grandaddy's boat was named *Coot*, but I still like *Eel* better. You know, how they slip through the water and all."

"Yea, we know, Drake. What else could we name her? Seems like eels is everywhere, not just here. Course, so is canvasbacks and coots far as that goes."

Lottie Dryden had been listening to the conversation. "Some of them canoes had some right good names. There's the *Mystery*, the *Magic*, and all them. The *Flying Cloud* was a good one. Then there was all them "aland" names. The *Aland Bird* and the *Aland Blossom* and the *Aland Lark*. Story goes they was built someplace on Tilghman Aland. Anyway, they were right good names."

"You're right, Lottie. Them were good names. That twelve that beat us was just called the *Australia*. We could name ours the *Oxford* or the *Talbot* or *Choptank* or somethin'. Ought to be somethin' better though." Hoyt didn't know what that something was.

"I still think *Eel* is a good name. You know, how they slip through the water and all?"

John piped up, "Gawd damn it, Drake. Will you forget *Eel*? Ain't nobody likes *Eel* 'cept you and your father. Plus that, if our twelve meter slipped through the water like your daddy's *Eel*, we'd never git her to Australia. It'd take two days to git to Balmer. That's the slowest gawd damn boat ever been in a race. She'd start a hundred mile race with a clean bottom and by the time she'd finish she'd need haulin', varnishin', and the season would've changed. Your daddy never did the "Skippers" race cause he was afraid he wouldn't get back for Christmas. I don't want to hear nothin' more 'bout no eel."

"Still a good name." Drake sure liked that name. "Course, you could always use a turkle name. *Snapper* would be good, or *Diamond Back*. Course, I like *Eel*, but I ain't goin' to bring that name up no more. Guess you could name it *Jellyfish*." Everybody just took a deep breath in disgust. Drake had had a few too many longnecks.

"You know what we got around here and they ain't nowhere else?" Hambden Martin asked, "What we got is somethin' that can go through the water like a fish and when he wants to, he can fight like a bear just like our boat's going to do. What we got that ain't nowhere else is a muskrat. Let's name her *Muskrat*."

John Dryden thought it was an excellent idea. A muskrat was strickly Eastern Shore. "What you think boys?" John put it up for a vote. "All those in favor?" He raised his longneck and everybody except Drake agreed.

If their twelve meter was ever built and it was okay with Samuel E. Johnson III, they'd name her *Muskrat*.

John went to the cooler and got a round of Budweiser longnecks. "Here's to the *Muskrat* and bringing back the cup!"

Everybody was jubilant. "Hooray! Hooray!" Everybody except Drake that is.

"I still like *Eel*. You know, how they slip through the water and all."

"Oh shut up, Drake!"

What a wonderful night it had been. The boys from Oxford were going to take a shot at building a twelve meter and go for the America's Cup. And why not? Some of the best sailors on the bay were from Oxford. Why couldn't they muster a crew as good as or better than anyone else's? They would have something no one else would have. They would have the *Muskrat* and hidden in the *Muskrat* would be the secret.

After a couple of hours of further discussion, it was time to call it a night. It was late and some of the boys had a pretty good hike home through the snow. The group broke up and headed out.

Chapter Two

John Dryden and Hoyt Crane always got up early and wandered down to Brinkley's store for a hot cup of coffee. Mrs. Brinkley, better known as Myrt to all the locals, made the best coffee in town. The store was on the main street in the middle of Oxford and during the course of a day, nearly every person in town would come in at least once. Many people picked up their paper there. Some had their paper delivered, but to get all the news of the day you had to go to Brinkley's.

The store had an amazing variety of items that could be purchased. In addition to the soda counter where you could get anything from wonderful ice cream sundaes to penny candy, there were shelves of canned goods and a large selection of refrigerated items like sandwich meats and milk. At the rear of the store was a selection of clothes including shirts and gloves. One of the most popular items was the khaki hats that all the watermen wore.

Obscure items were well hidden in little nooks and crannies all over the store. Myrt knew where everthing was. If you wanted an oyster knife or a can opener or a Phillips head screwdriver, she could find it for you. It was a wonderful place.

At six in the morning, you would find a dozen or so watermen gathered at Brinkley's to exchange stories, talk about what weather to expect for the day, and to fill their thermoses with Myrt's coffee. It was a popular meeting place.

The men met at Brinkley's in the morning and at Dryden's at day's end.

John Dryden and Hoyt Crane wandered in about six-thirty. It had snowed all night and there were fourteen inches of the white stuff on the ground. The aroma of the coffee filled the air as they joined a half dozen or so watermen talking about whether or not they were going tonging. Most didn't feel there'd be a market. No trucks could get out of town with their catch and the oysters would freeze if left in their boats overnight.

John and Hoyt both got their coffee. "I'm sure Nick Benson ain't up yet. Let's wait awhile and give him a call. Hoyt, do you think he'll do it?"

"John, Nick would be a fool not to do it as long as Sam Johnson is willing to pay for it."

"Nick's the only guy Sam Johnson would consider to build the *Muskrat*. He's the only man alive who knows the secret. Maybe John Allen knows it by now, but I ain't sure."

John Allen was a master builder just like his dad and grandad Ralph. They were lucky that Nick was still alive to oversee the project. That would mean a lot to Samuel E. Johnson III.

Nick's yard, still called "Ralph's Boatyard", was located on the south side of Cemetery Cove. As you stood at the railway and looked across Cemetery Cove, you could see a beautiful farm called Plimhimmon. To the right of the railway was the local Cemetery and to the left was a little pine thicket and beyond that was Nick's house. John Allen had a place in town on South Street.

The yard itself consisted of an old wood building about eighty feet long and maybe twenty-five feet wide. The railway ran right up into the building, which was painted red like most of the yards around. Above the double doors on the water side over the railway was printed out in big white letters, "Ralph's Boatyard Est. 1897".

Inside the building on each side was a long workbench piled with tools of every description. How anybody could find a particular tool nobody will ever know. On the end of the building, away from the water, there were two large saws. The dirt floor was covered with several inches of sawdust and shavings. There was a little room just off the main part of the building which housed a small office and a head. The only other building was simply a pole shed where they kept their lumber dry. On either side of the railway was a dock going out about one hundred fifty feet with several boat slips.

The property was completely fenced in, and the only access from land was through a large double gate near the Oxford road behind the local liquor store.

A Mr. William H. Bateman owned the big farm across from the yard, and in the winter he took hunting parties to hunt Canada geese. Every once in awhile a crippled goose would end up in the cove. Mr. Bateman never shot the cove, so John Allen would get his skiff and retrieve the cripple. He would bring it back and put it inside the fence and feed it. Over the years, he had acquired fourteen geese. Those geese were the best watchdogs ever seen. When somebody would open those gates they all would honk so loud no one could hear themselves think. Old Man Nick would come out and clap his hands and they'd quiet down.

At 7:30, John Dryden and Hoyt Crane called Nick and said they'd like to stop over. Nick said that's fine and to come on. They went by boat because of all the snow. John and Hoyt walked down Market Street to the public dock, where Hoyt had a boat, and went across the creek. As they approached "Ralph's

Boatyard," they saw John Allen shovelling out one of the boats. "That's good that John Allen's here," John said.

They called to him to come up to the house. "I'll be right up soon as I git the snow out of this bucket," he said. "You go on up."

When they entered the yard, the geese made a huge noise. Nick greeted them at the door.

"Sit down, boys. How about a cup of coffee?"

"Thanks, Nick."

They made their coffees and John Allen joined the group.

"What's on your mind, boys?" asked Nick.

Hoyt started the explanation. "Nick, you and your son are by far the best boat builders on the east coast. You have built the best and fastest boats ever to hit the water, just like your dad Ralph did and his dad before him. Nobody 'cept you boys knew why these boats go like they do."

"That ain't all, bunky. Ain't nobody gonna know. The only person I ever told was John Allen, and if you think I'm gonna tell you, then you're dumber than a gawd damn soft crab. The next person I tell is gonna be St. Peter, and I ain't tellin' him right off."

"Nick! Nick! Settle down now. I ain't here to learn your secret. What John and I came over here for is to see if you would build us a boat."

"What kind of boat you talkin' about Hoyt?" The old man asked.

"A twelve meter Nick. One of them twelve meters."

"You are dumber than a soft crab! Shee-it! You're dumber than a gawd damn soft crab and clam both! Build you and John a twelve meter? John, you been drinkin'?"

John Dryden didn't understand. They both knew Nick and John Allen since they were little boys. There were never any

36

problems.

"Why won't you build us a boat, Nick?"

"Boys, I've known both of you since before you put your first oars in the water. I like you both. But you're talkin' like you ain't got but **one** oar in the water now. Do you know what a twelve meter would cost to build? John, it would cost more than every longneck beer you'd ever see in three lifetimes. You boys can't afford no twelve meter. I'd love to build one of them boats, but I'll tell you one thing, it would be the most expensive boat ever come down my railway. If I built it for you, it would be the last thing come down my railway too. Somebody else would own her and I'd be broke."

"Nick, you don't understand. We ain't gonna pay for the boat."

"So you admit you ain't got the money. You got a lot of nerve comin' over here askin' me to build you a boat and admittin' you ain't goin' to pay for it."

"Wait Nick, you don't understand. We're gonna get Samuel E. Johnson III to foot the bill. Would you build it for Sam?"

Nick leaned back in his chair, and rubbing his chin, slowly looked up to the ceiling. He then looked at John Allen who hadn't said a word. John Allen looked at his dad and gave him a wink.

"They'll be some terms to nail down boys, and there will have to be one condition, but if Sam agrees to pay for it, we'll build your boat for you. I ain't never started a boat without 50% of the cost in the bank—**my** bank. When it's half done, I want the balance. If it goes over the agreed price by up to 15%, there ain't no penalty. These big boats are hard to figure sometimes. If it's above 15%, I'll work for the cost of the materials to finish it if it takes a year. If I'm under the agreed price, I git a $10,000 bonus. Believe me, a $10,000 bonus on the cost of a bucket like

37

that ain't nothin'. I can go over this with Sam.

"Now the condition. You boys know I got a secret to my boats. From the day I start building, the only two people allowed in my yard, 'cept my crew, are me and John Allen. Samuel E. Johnson, III has been trying to figure what the secret is for over fifty years, ever since my father built the *'Maggie P.'* He ain't gonna come here for seven months, him or nobody. It will be tempting for him to get a peek. You know Sam as well as I do. He told somebody once he'd spend his last dime on findin' out what the secret was. He's got to agree to that. Even if he does agree, I won't really trust him. Now just between us, John Allen and I have wanted to build a twelve meter for years. We'll do some different things that will be obvious to everybody right away, but they can't know the secret. Ain't nobody can come here, you understand? You have to make sure Sam won't break that trust.

"Now boys, I said I wanted half down before I started. I'm sure that won't be a problem for Sam, but I want you boys to make gawd damn sure that he lives up to his part of the bargain. I want each of you to put up $5,000 when Sam puts his money down. Ain't nobody to know about it, not Sam or nobody. If somebody decides to come snoopin' around, and I catch 'em, you lose $5,000 each. Now if everybody lives up to the bargain, I'll give you your $10,000 back. That way I know you'll help me keep the secret.

"If you can promise me you'll do that, then I'll build your boat. Can you?"

John looked at Hoyt and took a deep breath. He also knew that Sam was not the most trustworthy man around. Hoyt broke out in a cold sweat. John looked back at old man Nick. "I promise, Nick. I promise."

They shook hands and headed for the dock. The geese

made such a racket, they could be heard all over town. John and Hoyt got in the boat and headed out.

"John, have we lost our gawd damn minds? The way I figure it, you and me are bettin' $10,000 that Samuel E. Johnson III is honest. I ain't so sure that's a good bet John."

"Hoyt, if we don't, there'll never be a *Muskrat*."

"I guess you're right. Let's give Sam a call. Maybe we can see him later."

They tied the boat up and went to Hoyt's house to call Sam. It was hard walking in the snow.

Hoyt lived on Morris Street not far from Brinkley's store. They went in and John got Sam on the phone.

"Sam, this is John Dryden."

"Hello, John. What can I do for you?"

"Sam, I'm here at Hoyt Crane's house and we were wonderin' if we could come up and talk to you about somethin' this afternoon. Are you going to be around?"

"Hell yes, I'll be here. I'm snowed in. How in Christ's name are you going to get here? We got over a foot of snow."

"Hoyt's boat is runnin'. We can come up in that."

"Can't you tell me what this is all about over the phone John?"

"Well it's a..., well it's about *Muskrat*."

"About a muskrat! Have you boys been drinking?"

"No, Sam. I'll explain it all when we get there. Would one-thirty be okay?"

"Yes, I'll see you at one-thirty. Muskrat? What the..." Click, John hung up.

The boys got a bite to eat, bundled up again, and headed for Hoyt's boat. They arrived at Sam's about one-forty-five and walked up to the house. They were greeted at the door by a maid. She was a very pleasant black woman in her early sixties.

She wore a white uniform and was very much overweight.

"Mr. Johnson is expectin' ya. Come right this way." She showed them to the den where Samuel E. Johnson, III sat in a huge leather chair by a roaring fire, smoking a large cigar. His snow white hair almost glowed against the red leather chair. The den was gorgeous with several beautiful models decorating the dark cherry paneled walls. Over the mantel was an oil painting of one of his former yachts, *Dora*, coming out of the fog at Brenton Reef light. On either side of the fireplace were book cases. The smell of cigar smoke filled the room.

"Come in, boys. How about a little toddy to warm your bones?"

"That sounds right nice. Thanks, Sam." John was chilled after the boat ride.

"Thanks," added Hoyt.

After they had gotten their drinks, they sat down in front of the roaring fire.

"Now, boys, what's this about some muskrat?"

"Well, Sam, the *Muskrat* is really a boat. It all started last night over a few beers at the bar. It was Hoyt and me, Drake Cochran, and a bunch of other people..."

John described what they proposed to do in every detail. Sam didn't say a word. He listened very intently; every once in awhile drawing a long puff from his cigar and looking up toward the oil painting of *Dora*. Hoyt didn't say a word either. He was studying Sam's face, trying to figure out what his reaction was going to be. He was very nervous.

John talked for a good half hour. Finally he said, "So that's it, Sam. We can put together the best crew ever from our local boys. Hoyt here has agreed to skipper and as you know, he's one of the best. Nick and John Allen Benson will build the boat with them conditions. We got everything 'cept the money.

What do ya think, Sam?"

Hoyt was on the edge of his seat by now, taking huge gulps from his glass of bourbon. John anxiously awaited Sam's reply.

Sam never changed his expression. He looked John in the eye and took a long drag from his cigar, looked up at the ceiling and slowly exhaled. Then, without saying a word, he stood and left the room, shutting the door behind him.

"He ain't gonna do it, John. Gawd damn it, he ain't gonna do it. After all this. Shee-it! Been runnin' around in the snow all day. Froze my ass off in the gawd damn boat coming up here and he don't say yes, no, kiss my ass or nothin'."

"Settle down now, Hoyt. He ain't said no yet. Come on, let's sneak another drink. I ain't never had bourbon like this before. Least we'll get a couple a free drinks of this fancy stuff."

It was a good twenty minutes before Sam returned. He opened the door, went over and poured himself a drink, and stood facing the boys in front of the fireplace. Hoyt and John were as nervous as squirrels.

Sam held his drink up and said, "Here's to the *Muskrat* and getting that cup back!"

John was ecstatic, "To the *Muskrat*!" He turned to Hoyt for another toast. Hoyt was in tears, but managed to get another gulp down.

"Shee-it, Hoyt, stop that crying. Twelve meter skippers ain't supposed to cry."

The three men talked for at least two hours about some of the possible crew and discussed some of the details before the boys headed down the river. Sam walked them to the door. As they were leaving, Hoyt asked, "Sam, it ain't none of my business, but I'm wonderin' what you was doin' when you left the room."

" I made a couple of phone calls, Hoyt. First, I called an old friend of mine who has been involved with twelve meters for years. He said, 'Go for it you old poop. There may not be any twelves in heaven.' He also agreed to meet Nick and me in Newport in a few days. I want you to go, too. There are several twelves there now. It'd be good for us to see 'em. Then I called Nick Benson to check on some of the details."

"Boy, you had me scared for a minute there," Hoyt said.

As they said goodbye, John took Sam by the arm. "Nick's real serious about us staying away from the yard."

"Don't worry about that, John. I'll have a lot invested in the boat, but it's only money." The boys headed down for the dock.

Hoyt whispered to John, "Easy for him to say. Where in the hell are we gonna git $10,000?"

"I don't know Hoyt, but I know one thing.... We're gettin' ready to build a twelve. The boys down to the bar are really gonna be excited."

They boarded the boat and headed for Oxford. It was a pleasant trip home. There wasn't a breath of air and the snow-covered shores were lovely. They thought of the excitement ahead as they nipped a little brandy. A lot had happened in the last twenty-four hours. To think, no one had even heard of the *Muskrat* when the snow started Tuesday morning.

The celebration at Dryden's went on well into the next morning. No one could believe that a twelve meter was going to be built in Oxford and end up racing half way around the world sailed by a bunch of local yokels. But, why not? Old man Nick was a great boat builder, Hoyt was a great skipper, and there wasn't a better group of sailors around than the boys that lived right there.

Friday afternoon John Dryden got a call from Samuel E. Johnson III. "John, this is Sam. I want you and Hoyt to go with Nick and me to Newport Monday morning. We're going to meet my friend, Ewing Brown. He's the one that knows twelve meters in and out. Nick needs to talk to him about the building formula. There are three twelves there he can study. One is in the water with her rig in it. He might get some ideas. We'll take my big wagon. Can you get someone to drive?"

"Sure, Sam, no problem. How long will we be there?"

"I figure we'll be there a day or two. I'll have my secretary make the necessary arrangements. Be at my house at ten o'clock Monday morning."

"See you then, Sam. If there are any hitches, I'll let you know. If you don't hear from me, we'll be there at ten."

"Oh, John, don't worry about money, I'll take care of that. And John, make sure everybody brings their church clothes. You understand?"

"Yeah, Sam. I understand."

Sam called Hoyt and told him of the plan. He then called Nick to confirm things and found out the reason that John Allen wasn't going was because of the business. It wouldn't be necessary anyway. It might be better to just have Nick. Then John Allen would have to do it Nick's way.

He thought about a driver. The only person he could come up with was Drake Cochran. He would be in that night and he'd line him up.

"Gawd damn if he won't be somethin' in Newport." He thought to himself.

They arrived at Sam's estate at ten Monday morning; packed the wagon, and headed for Newport, Rhode Island. As they headed up the road, the conversation turned to crew selection.

"Who do you have in mind for tactician, Hoyt?"

"I'm not sure, Sam, but I think Hambden could do it. He can spot a wind shift same as an osprey spots a trout. I seen him

round the Choptank light once a quarter mile behind Capt'n
Lenny Roth. They was headin' up the Tred Avon and the air
was shifty as a Balmer lawyer. Well Hambden never missed
neither shift. I thought he'd wear out his tiller, let alone his
crew. By the time he got to the club, he had Captn' Lenny by ten
boat lengths. He left that boy scratchin' his head. He's good
Sam."

"Now, these boats are big, Hoyt. You'll need some strong
men to do the grinding. Twelves are famous for tacking duels
and they'll wear a man down."

"Shee-it, Sam! You go down to Dryden's Saturday night
and look them tongers over. Gawd damn, them boys could
start a tackin' duel before breakfast and at sundown stop
grindin' an' eat the winches. Won't be neither boat with better
grinders than what we'll muster. Bradley and Herbert are
hankerin' to go. Drake, you'll do it won't you?"

"Gawd damn right I'll do it."

"I bet Mark Litty woul, too. Don't you worry 'bout grinders, I'll tell you, we'll have plenty of grinders."

"I guess you're right, Hoyt. Those boys can handle that.
What about the cockpit?"

"Well, the best main trimmer around is that girl that teaches
sailin' down to the yacht club. Allison Deemer's her name. She
can git them tell tales a flyin' when it's dish pan ca'm. Plus that
we need somethin' pretty to look at with the rest of the crew
we're takin'.

"Bailey Shultz is good on sail trim. He's done an awful lot
of racin' all over. He can call a spinnaker 'bout anything he
wants.

"Glenn Parrot and Pete Dillon are good men aft. Glenn and
Pete have done a bunch of Bermuda and Trans-Atlantics.

"Schuyler Mattingly and Jim Firth are crackerjack boys on

the pointy end. Vaughn Downes is good, too. That Jimmy Firth can crawl up a head stay like a squirrel up a tree. I seen him go up a sixty foot spar in thirty knots with neither chair. Them boys can jibe a chute in their sleep.

"We'll have a good crew, Sam, a damn good crew."

"How about sails, Hoyt? Is North the best? There are so many sailmakers. There's North, Hood, Sobstad, Ulmer-Kolius. It goes on and on."

"Sam, you ain't gonna believe this, but there ain't neither of 'em any better than Downes Hackett back in Oxford. Downes can cut a sail pretty as a longneck in shaved ice. Might as well keep it local Sam. Ain't gonna hurt nothin' and that way ain't nobody to know what we're up to."

Downes Hackett had a sail loft on Bank Street. He was a black man who had learned his trade as a child from one of the best sailmakers ever; Wayne Pritchett. Downes had made sails for many of the racing boats that dominated racing on the Chesapeake.

They arrived at the Treadway Hotel in Newport at six o'clock. Sam's friend, Commodore Ewing Brown, was waiting for them in the lobby. The Commodore had an 85-foot motor sailer and insisted that the boys stay aboard. After introducing Commodore Brown to everyone, Sam suggested the boys take their things to the boat and relax, while he and Nick had a drink or two at the bar with the Commodore.

The three men found a small table at the bar, and after a brief period of small talk, directed their thoughts to twelve meters. Commodore Brown had served on the New York Yacht Club Race Committee during several challenges for the Cup. This year he headed a syndicate that built a twelve. He knew the ins and outs of building and campaigning a boat.

Old man Nick Benson had studied the twelve meter formula in some depth and had a good understanding of what could and couldn't be done. The rules are somewhat complicated, however. Even though he knew the rules pretty well, Nick still had many questions to ask.

The Commodore spoke. "Mr. Benson, in our last defense of the America's Cup, our boats were sailed very well. All of our yachts could produce about equal speeds. The Aussies sailed their boat well too, but they did more. They made a breakthrough in design. That's what we have to do, Mr. Benson. The sad part is that they are ahead of us."

Old man Nick looked the Commodore in the eyes. "I ain't so sure 'bout that, Commodore. Maybe we know somethin' they don't."

Nick held up his glass of beer and gave Sam Johnson a wink. "Here's to gettin' that cup, Commodore. Let's drink to the *Muskrat* ."

"That's a most unusual name for a twelve meter yacht, Mr. Benson."

"They'll be somethin' 'bout our twelve that'll be a gawd damn site more unusual than her name, Commodore. You can bet your burgee on that." Nick took the last sip of his beer, obviously very pleased with the answers the Commodore had given.

It didn't take Hoyt and the rest of the boys more than five minutes to find the Black Pearl bar after they left Sam, Nick and the Commodore. They put their gear aboard the *Explorer* and went straight to the bar. There they downed round after round of Budweiser longnecks and were beginning to get into a rather drunken state.

At about eight o'clock, the boys recognized a man stumbling into the Black Pearl. He was Franklin Arthurs from Easton. He had his fifty-two foot yawl, *Whisper*, at the Newport

Off-Shore Boatyard having extensive work done on its interior. Franklin was three sheets to the wind.

"Hello boys. Bartender, get these boys a drink on me." Franklin stumbled over and sat down.

"What brings you to Newport, Hoyt?"

Hoyt Crane explained and Franklin got real excited.

"That's the greatest news I've ever heard. Let's celebrate. I'm buying you all dinner at Christies."

Christies is a lovely restaurant on the Newport Harbor. The food is good and the prices high. The boys weren't about to turn Franklin's offer down. And so Hoyt, John Dryden and Drake Cochran stumbled down the street to Christies following Franklin Arthurs, who could barely walk. Somehow all four men made it to the restaurant and, what was more amazing, were seated by the hostess.

When the waiter approached the table, Franklin slurred his instructions, "Man I would like to buy these men dinner. I am very hungry so take my order right now and come back for the rest. I'll have a thick slice of rare roast beef with lots of mashed potatoes and gravy. Hurry up with it and bring me a martini."

Hoyt thought Franklin was a little rude, "The hell with this, I'll go git us a beer at the bar if I can find it." He wandered off.

Drake was so disgusted with Franklin he said, "I'm gettin' out of here right now. We're all drunk and I ain't gettin' in no trouble."

The problem was Drake was so potted, instead of the front door, he went into the men's room. "First time I ever seen urinals in the middle of the street. Gawd damn!"

After about five minutes, John Dryden was wondering where Hoyt had gone with the beer. He left Franklin in a stupor at the table, barely able to hold up his head. John spotted Hoyt at the bar and made his way over.

"What the hell are you doin', Hoyt?"

"Gawd damn it, John. I've been all over this place and can't find no place to git a drink."

"Damn it, Hoyt. You're leanin' against the bar and been talkin' to the bartender. Now go sit down."

On his way back to the table, Hoyt wandered in the men's room.

"What the hell are you doin' just standin' in the middle of the men's room, Drake?"

"Gawd damn, Hoyt. I'm lost. I don't remember all these urinals in the street comin' over here."

"You're in the men's room, Drake. Come on, let's go eat."

John brought the beer back to the table and the three boys ordered dinner and another round. Franklin could hardly stay awake.

Shortly, the waitress arrived with Franklin's dinner. She put his plate in front of him on which was placed a beautiful thick juicy piece of roast beef, surrounded with a large mound of mashed potatoes, piled high with hot gravy.

Franklin looked down at the gorgeous meal and then with a blank stare, gazed at John directly across the table from him. Within a second or two, Franklin's head dropped. It turned as it went crashing into his plate, burying his left ear deep into the mound of potatoes and gravy. In spite of the temperature of the steaming food, Franklin didn't budge. What a place to pass out. Drake grabbed Franklin by the hair and lifted his head, slid the plate from under him, and then gently laid his head back on the table.

Soon the boys' dinner arrived. They explained to the waitress that their friend had been very ill recently and decided to take a rest. They ordered another round and began with their dinner.

Hoyt dug into his spaghetti dinner. "Pass the Palmer Johnson cheese, please." John chuckled.

After a short while, John noticed that Drake was having a hard time with his lobster. It seemed that he was eating not only the meat, but shells and everything. He was making a loud crunching sound, and John noticed a little blood running down the corner of his mouth.

"What the hell are you doing, Drake? You gotta pick the meat out. Your gums is bleedin'."

"Look at it, John! I ain't never seen a steak this rare before. Its tougher than hell. Son-of-a-bitch ain't cooked. Look how red it is, John."

"Gawd damn it Drake! That ain't no steak; it's a lobster, you dumb ass! No wonder your gums is bleedin'."

With some help from John, Drake finished his lobster. The boys had one for the road. Hoyt found Franklin's wallet and left his American Express card sticking up in the mashed potatoes. They left Franklin passed out at the table and headed for the Commodore's boat.

On the way back, Hoyt spotted a bar. He insisted they needed one more. John and Drake declined and went on as Hoyt went in.

On the way back to the *Explorer*, Drake and John spotted some pigeons walking just ahead of them down the sidewalk. They tried desperately to catch one to put in Hoyt's bunk. They were a sight for sore eyes, stumbling down the street around midnight, trying to catch a pigeon. Luckily, they weren't successful. The Commodore would be happy about that. They found the boat and within one minute both were snoring like crazy.

The Commodore, Sam and Old Man Nick had an early dinner and retired. They were going to inspect the

Commodore's twelve the next morning and wanted to be sharp.

At about 2:30, Hoyt thought he should get back to the boat. He paid his tab and went out to the street. He looked around and was confused as to which way to go.

There was an elderly man standing on the corner who obviously had sllugged down his share of booze. "Cap'n could you tell me how I would get to the Treadmill?"

The old man looked Hoyt in the eye, then he looked up the street toward the north. He studied it for a while, then he looked to the south. "Treadmill. Treadmill," he said softly to himself.

Then he looked up the street to the west and paused, and he did the same to the east. This took at least a minute.

"Mister," he finally said, "I don't believe you can get there from here. You better go somewhere else and start. This is a hard place to get out of."

Hoyt just shrugged his shoulders, picked a street, and started walking. The further he walked, the more lost he got and the worse he felt. At about 3:30, Hoyt hailed a cab and got in.

"Where to, sir?"

"Take me to my boat, Capt'n."

"Where's your boat, sir?"

"What the hell do you think I hired you for? I don't know where my gawd damn boat is."

"Sir, there are hundreds of boats in Newport!"

"I don't care if there are ten million. I only want you to take me to one!"

After much discussion and patience on the part of the cabby, they found the *Explorer*. As it turned out, when Hoyt got into the taxi, they were one block from the boat. The taxi fare was $25.

He walked down the dock in front of the Treadway, and looked down at the *Explorer*. As he was stepping aboard he realized that the tide had gone out. When he had left the boat, it was level with the dock. It now was six feet below, and that's how far Hoyt was falling. When he hit the deck he unfortunately also hit a staunchion with his left arm. He heard a snap. The arm was broken.

The only lucky thing was that he was on the forward end of the boat and only woke up John, Drake and the boat Captain.

John looked at Hoyt laying on the deck. "Hoyt, you're doin' alright on your flyin', but if you don't brush up on your landin's, you're gonna kill yourself."

"Go to hell, John!"

They bandaged his arm and put him in his bunk. They would worry about Hoyt later, after all, it was four-thirty in the morning.

Commodore Ewing Brown was sitting in the cockpit having a cup of coffee when Sam Johnson appeared at the companionway. It was seven-thirty.

"Good morning, Commodore."

"Good morning, Sam. Have Victor get you a coffee. It's chilly."

Victor was the captain aboard the *Explorer*.

"When did the boys get in last night, Victor?" Sam inquired.

"I can't say when John and Drake came back. I was asleep. But Hoyt dropped in kind of late."

John and Drake appeared around ten of eight and grabbed a coffee and joined the Commodore and Sam. At a couple of minutes to eight, the Commodore went below and Victor came up with the ensign. As eight o'clock approached, the Commodore barked out numbers below as if a race were to start. "Five, four, three, two, one, Colors!"

The instant the Commodore yelled, "Colors," Victor jammed the flag staff in its holder and as quickly as possible had the ensign flapping in the breeze. It was 0800 hours.

"Gawd damn, John, he runs this boat like my DI ran boot camp. I hope Hoyt didn't tear up anything when he hit."

"Shut up, Drake!" John elbowed him in the side.

"Where's Hoyt?"

"Oh uh, Sam, he ain't feelin' real good this mornin'. Seems like he took a spill last night gettin' aboard. I ain't sure he didn't break his arm."

They arranged for a cab and John took Hoyt to the Newport Hospital. The plan was to have Hoyt's arm looked after and to meet the rest of them at Williams and Manchester Boatyard to see the Commodore's twelve meter at eleven-thirty.

Back aboard the *Explorer*, Victor prepared a lovely breakfast for the Commodore and his guests. After a leisurely meal, they wandered down the street toward the boatyard. At eleven-thirty, they stepped aboard the *Golden Eagle* .

The *Eagle* was the twelve meter built by Commodore Ewing Brown's syndicate. She was Sparklin and Stepen's latest. Her aluminum hull glistened in the harbor as John and Hoyt walked down the dock and joined the group. Hoyt's arm was in a cast. It was broken just above the wrist.

"This is the latest design, Sam." The Commodore was very proud of the new twelve.

"She's quite a machine, Commodore. I'm impressed with the electronics. We certainly are living in the computer age." Sam said.

Drake punched John in the ribs. "Shee-it. Gawdamn bucket looks like a space ship with all them funny dials. Which one's the microwave."

"Shut up Drake. The Commodore might hear ya."

"Look, John, she's got two wheels to her. How in Christ's name can two people steer one boat at the same time? I guess the biggest man steerin' gets to go wherever he wants to."

"Gawd damn it, Drake, there ain't two helmsmen. She's got two wheels so the man steerin' can git to weather. Let's him move around and all."

"What's them two machines for up there with them handles in 'em, John?"

"They're coffee grinders, Drake. Four men can grind at the same time."

"Coffee grinders! You mean to tell me that boat's going to race having four men grindin' coffee? You can buy a little jar of instant to take that don't weigh nothin'."

"Dammit, Drake, they don't grind coffee. They're winches, you fool! They turn these drums on the deck."

As they went below, the Commodore and Sam were talking about the cost of a twelve. "We've got 1.6 million in the *Eagle*," the Commodore said.

Nick was suprised at the price. "That's a lot of money, Commodore. I can build one for a lot less than that."

Nick studied every inch of the boat, paying particular attention to the coffee grinder mechanisms below decks.

Drake stood below shaking his head. John was afraid he would open his mouth and make another stupid comment. His fear was well founded. Drake piped up, "Commodore. You got 1.6 million into her now. What will you have when she's finished?"

John punched him in the ribs, "Drake, will you please shut the hell up?"

The Commodore was a little embarrassed, but mostly humored. "She *is* finished, Mr. Cochran."

Drake whispered to John, "Don't look finished to me. Ain't no bunks or galley. Hell, she's got coffee grinders, but no place to put the pot."

John cracked him in the ribs again. "Will you shut up, Drake? They don't live on twelves. They just build 'em to race. Now don't say nothin'. Just look!"

Old man Nick Benson was enjoying the tour on *Golden Eagle*. His mind was going a mile a minute. Nick's genius when it came to boat building was already generating ideas for the *Muskrat* . Nick had a lot of questions about weight ratios with her underbelly and keel.

In spite of a huge hangover, and a now painful arm, Hoyt was very impressed. He'd love to take her out and try her. He thought to himself, "She must be awfully fast; to think I'll be racing against her in the trials." He wondered how the *Muskrat* would fare against a state of the art machine like the *Golden Eagle* .

"Look, John, look at my knife. Hardest wood I ever seen. Bent my good pocket knife. What the hell kind a wood is she made of, John?"

"She ain't made of no wood, Drake. She's aluminized or however you say it. She's metal."

"Metal? You mean this bucket's made of metal? Well at least she won't dry rot. What do you do about the rust and all? I guess they paint her with that Rustoleum®. You can get any color now. I wouldn't want to be in no lightnin' squall on her, I can tell you that. She'd light up like a Christmas tree. I wonder how they patch her if she get's a hole or somethin'. Must keep a right smart supply of Reynolds' Wrap® around here I guess."

"Drake, if you don't keep your mouth shut, I'm gonna smack you up long side your head."

Drake just couldn't get over the *Golden Eagle* .

"I'll tell you one thing, John. They may try to sail this thing to Australia, but I wouldn't sail across Town Creek on her."

"I'm gettin' ready to smack the shit out of you, Drake. I mean it."

John meant it too. Enough was enough.

Sam spoke, "Commodore, I can't thank you enough for showing us the *Eagle*. I'm sure you're very proud. We're proud to be on the same team with you. After all, we're all trying to get back our cup. You can rest assured, the competition between *Muskrat* and *Eagle* will be friendly competition."

"I'm sure it will Sam! It was my pleasure to show her to you."

Hoyt thought to himself, "Bullshit! I ain't never been friendly to nobody on no race course, and I ain't gonna start now. I like 'em at the bar, but I hate 'em at the line."

Deep down inside, the Commodore wasn't too concerned about the *Muskrat*. They'd never be able to do what Sparklin and Stepens and Thalmer Johnson had done. He welcomed the interest in getting the cup back, but after looking Sam's group over, he thought Sam might be wasting a lot of money.

Sam thought to himself that he had better get the boys back to Oxford, especially Hoyt. If he let Hoyt stay much longer, he'd loose his skipper. He'd already lost an arm. Sam said goodbye to Commodore Ewing Brown, packed up the wagon, and headed back to the Eastern Shore.

Old man Nick Benson couldn't wait to get back and start on the *Muskrat*. He was very excited.

Sam lit a cigar and looked at Nick. "Well, what do you think? The *Golden Eagle* is quite a machine isn't she?"

"Yea, she's alright, Sam. But I'll tell you one thing. From what I seen, I don't think she's gonna be able to pack with the *'Rat* ."

Chapter Three

When they got home Nick started gathering the materials to build the *Muskrat*.. Hoyt and John borrowed $10,000 from the local bank, and Samuel E. Johnson III put up $600,000.

On February the third, old man Nick and John Allen closed the gates and started to build the twelve meter. No one was to come in the yard for six months, not until August first.

That day was to be the day Muskrat would be launched. She would then be taken to the Oxford Boatyard where her spars and rigging were being made. Downes Hackett would have the sails ready, and if possible, they would enter a race or two before shipping to Australia for the October trials. There was no time to waste. Their project started late, but there was no other way.

Old man Nick and John Allen had a powerful task before them. Nick suggested to Sam that the *Muskrat* grinders, the four boys he chose to work the grinders, work out all summer in rowing shells. Sam provided the shells, and every morning, there were four men rowing up and down Town Creek and when weather permitted, out into the Tred Avon River.

Hoyt Crane was having a few longnecks at Dryden's one evening in June. It was getting dark and he could see the shed light at Ralph's Boatyard.

"John, I wonder what she looks like. Only eight more weeks to the launch. I'd give anything to be in that shed right now."

"If you was in that shed right now, one gawd damn thing you'd be givin' away is my ass, cause I would have lost it! You too! You got $5,000 to throw away? I ain't!"

Hoyt laughed. "You're right about that. I wish school was startin' tomorrow instead of gettin' out. It might keep some of them wild kids busy. They scare me, Hoyt. Takes one kid caught over there and we're out ten grand."

John agreed, "What scares me is if somebody wants to know the secret, they'd wait 'til about now to try to find out. No sense in peekin' when Nick's startin' a boat. Ain't nothin' to see."

"Gawd damn, John, don't talk like that. You know, I can't believe Sam ain't even talked about the secret. That man's wanted to know that secret all his life and he ain't said neither word about it. Don't make sense. Somethin's wrong."

"It does seem kind'a fishy."

"What do you think the secret is John?"

"Hoyt, ain't nobody knows 'cept them two and their crew at the yard. I bet it's somethin' 'bout her belly. Kinda' like that Aussie boat. I can't wait to see her though. To think that she's sittin' in that shed right now."

The *Muskrat* was the topic of conversation all over town. From six in the morning at Brinkley's until closing time at Dryden's, the conversation centered around the *Muskrat* and the Benson boy's secret. Everyone wondered if it was at all possible for the boat to be competitive with the other twelves. Could Nick Benson design and build a fast twelve and not violate any of the rules? The whole town was waiting for the launching.

There wasn't an afternoon or evening that went by without a group at Dryden's gazing at Ralph's Boatyard, speculating about what would happen over the next few months. This was without question the most exciting thing ever to take place in the little town of Oxford. To dream that on a snowy night only five months earlier, a conversation about the skipjack *Maggie P,.* could trigger the building of a twelve meter in Oxford, Maryland. It was hard to believe, but it was true. As the time drew nearer to the day of launching, the excitement grew.

It was July 7, about eleven-thirty in the evening, and business was slow. After John Dryden cleaned up the bar he went out to the deck which overlooked Town Creek and sat down to enjoy a night cap. It was overcast, but the temperature was mild, and a nice breeze was funneling up the creek.

As he sat there, all of a sudden he heard a thunderous sound from across the creek that made him explode out of his chair. He was terrified. This couldn't be happening. The sound was coming from Ralph's Boatyard and what he heard were fourteen honking geese.

John ran inside the bar and called Hoyt, "Hoyt! The geese! The geese! I heard the geese!"

"John, are you drunk? What the hell are you so gawd damn excited about? Ain't you heard a goose before?"

"Gawd damn it Hoyt! They're the geese at Ralph's Boatyard! Somebody's over there spookin' around! Get goin', I'll meet you there!"

"Oh no! My $5,000...." Click!

John jumped in his car and tore down Tilghman Street, heading for the yard. He went through the stop sign at Morris Street, squealing his tires and nearly hitting a little Honda Accord, as he was making a left turn. Unfortunately, the town cop, Walter, was in front of the Robert Morris Inn, heading toward the ferry dock. He saw John in his rear view mirror and made a "U" turn. Walter threw on his siren and bubble gum machine. The chase was on.

Hoyt was just getting in his car when John flew by with the

town cop in hot pursuit. Hoyt took off. He himself had tried to call Walter, and when he didn't reach him, he called the fire department. As the three cars raced out of town, the cop chasing John, and Hoyt chasing the cop, the fire whistle blew.

Walter caught John and was right on his rear bumper when John made his turn into the boatyard lane. John's move caught Walter unaware. As the cop car made it's left, it rolled over into Bateman's corn field. When it finally came to a stop, the car ended up on its side, siren and blinking lights still going strong. Hoyt made the turn and stopped to see if Walter was all right. He jumped out and found Walter among the corn stalks. Walter was not hurt, but he was covered from head to toe with mud and his shirt was badly torn. It was quite a sight.

Meanwhile, the firemen had answered the siren and were on their way with three trucks followed by the ambulance. It looked like the Fourth of July coming up the Oxford Road. Following that procession were at least fifteen cars filled with curiosity seekers. Whenever the siren sounded, half the town turned out to see what was going on.

By the time Hoyt got Walter back to his car, the fire trucks and ambulance were there. Hoyt's car was blocking them. Hoyt explained to Walter about the intruder as they headed toward the yard.

John was already there, running around the outside of the fence trying to decide what to do. He couldn't go inside. If he did, he'd break his promise and lose his $5,000 for sure. He kept looking inside the fence, but couldn't make out anything because of the darkness. The geese were still making a terrible racket. John looked out toward the fire trucks and couldn't believe his eyes. He saw Hoyt's car followed by three fire trucks, the ambulance, and a parade of headlights plus something blinking in the middle of the cornfield.

Hoyt barrelled up to the front gate. He and Walter jumped out. Hoyt ran to get Nick Benson. Walter drew his gun and ran to the gate. He was trying to open it when from out of nowhere someone pounced on him and threw him to the ground. As he went down his gun flew from his mud filled hand and landed several feet away.

"Whoever this was, had to be big and strong," thought Walter.

As they were wrestling on the ground, the fire trucks and ambulance arrived followed by a stream of private cars. The place was in a tremendous turmoil. The sirens were wailing, the lights were blinking, and the fourteen Canada geese were honking their hearts out.

Walter yelled to the firemen, "Turn on your flood lights! Get this son-of-a-bitch off me!"

As Hoyt and old man Nick approached the front gate, the floodlights from all three trucks came on at the same time. They saw five firemen pulling John Dryden and the cop apart.

"What the hell are you doin', John?" Walter was furious.

"I was afraid you was goin' inside the gate, Walter. Ain't nobody supposed to be inside that gate 'cept John Allen and their men."

"Well, there's got to be someone inside, John. How in hell we gonna find him if somebody doesn't go in?"

"Git your loud speaker, Walter. Tell him to come out here. He can't hide in there forever and he sure as hell ain't gonna sneak out the way this place is lit up."

"John, do you see that red and blue blinking light in the middle of that field out there?"

"What is *that*, Walter?"

"That's where my hailer is, John. It's in what used to be my police car. Now I'm going in there!"

"I've got a hailer." Davey Abbott, the Fire Chief, reached in the truck and handed Walter a loud speaker.

Walter took the hailer, and raising it to his mouth, faced the lit up shed. "Come out with your hands up! You are surrounded!"

Nothing happened.

"You are surrounded! Give up! You will not be harmed! Come out with your hands up!"

Still nothing happened.

"Someone's got to go in, John." Walter was ready.

"Nick, would you care if Walter went in there?" Hoyt asked.

"I'll go in myself, Hoyt. Walter, give me your gun."

Old man Nick opened the gate and went to the door of the shed. He slowly and carefully opened the door and leaving it open, went inside. Everyone was very much concerned about the old man.

"We'd better go in with him." Walter said to John.

"Let's wait another minute, Walter."

In a few seconds, the lights went on inside the shed.

"Git the hell out of here you devil." Old man Nick had found him.

"Let's go, John." Walter and John were opening the gate to make sure Nick was okay when suddenly they stopped. Everybody burst out laughing when they saw two raccoons coming out of Nick's boat shed. They turned the corner and disappeared into the night.

Nick appeared at the door grinning from ear to ear. As he approached the main gate, he looked at John. "Guess them coons are worth 'bout $5,000 a piece ain't they?"

Walter was beside himself. "Gawd damn you, John Dryden! You started all this. Look what you've done. Got half the town out of bed. Brung out the fire department, ambulance and all; tore up half a cornfield and wrecked my new police car, ruined my uniform and lost my gun, all over two racoons. John, I'm arresting you for speedin' and reckless drivin'. I ain't wasting the whole night for nothin'."

John didn't care. The fine was a lot less than $5,000. If he could just hang on for seventeen more days, the *Muskrat* would be launched and he and Hoyt would get their $5,000 back.

On July 15, Hoyt got a phone call. "Hoyt, Sam Johnson. I want you to gather up the entire crew and John Dryden. We are going to have a meeting at the Tred Avon Yacht Club tonight at eight o'clock. I have to go over some details and Nick Benson says he has some very important developments to discuss."

"I'll round'em up, Sam."

Hoyt got everyone lined up, and at eight o'clock, they gathered at the Club. This was strictly a business meeting. The men took their seats around a large table in front of the fireplace. Nick and Sam were at the head of the table.

Sam stood up. "Thank you for coming down here tonight. I want to bring you up to date on some details and scheduling.

"As you know, arrangements have been made to fly all of us to Perth, September fifteenth. We will fly from BWI to San Francisco; then to Honolulu. From Honolulu we fly to Sidney, and then to Perth. *Muskrat* should arrive the eighteenth. That leaves very little time to get things together. We are at a distinct disadvantage. Every other twelve has been sailing for over a year. We'll only have eighteen days to put her together and get her going. The trials start October fifth.

"Our tender will be the *Oxford Queen* . You're familiar with her. She's that seventy-eight foot buy boat that Nick converted to a pleasure craft two years ago. She'll sleep fifteen.

"I want you boys to stay on her. That way you'll stay out of trouble until we either get eliminated or win. As I said, the round robin series starts October fifth for the challengers. On December twenty-eighth, they start the semi-finals and the challenger finals start January thirteenth. By January twenty-third the challenger will be chosen. I'd like to think it will be *Muskrat*. The actual America's Cup series starts January thirty-first.

"Now, arrangements have been made to fly your wives down on January twenty-second. We'll decide when to fly back depending on how we do. I'm prepared to stay until the end, of course. The ladies will stay in a hotel in Fremantel which is at the mouth of the Swan River. Perth on the other hand is way up the river. We'll keep our boats at Fremantle also.

"Now, boys, we've got our work cut out for us. The United States has seven syndicates alone. More than thirty new twelve meters have been built for this America's Cup Series. The United States is one of nine nations who will try to be named the challenger. Only then do we get a crack at getting the cup back.

"We have to fly the burgee of a yacht club located "on the arm of a sea". The Tred Avon Yacht Club has agreed to let us fly theirs.

"Hoyt tells me that you boys have kept up with your physical exercises, especially the four grinders with their work in the shells. Keep it up. It blows hard down there. You mark my word. It's going to be a bigger test on the crew than any previous America's Cup. Some of them are going to fatigue and mistakes will follow." Sam was dead right about that. There would be more wind, bigger seas, shorter legs and they had added two legs to the course. It would be quite a test for men and equipment.

"Our sails, believe it or not, are ready. It took a little doing and a couple of cases of whiskey, but Downes Hackett came through for us. Our spars and rigging are ready with spares. All in all we're in good shape. Nick Benson has some very important information to discuss about *Muskrat.*"

"Fellers, first off, the *Muskrat* is finished. We got her done a few days early. She looks real good. John Allen and I are right happy with her.

"Now, I'm goin' to slide her down the runway tonight, and take her over to the Oxford Boatyard. The boys are all set to meet at one in the mornin' to put her spar in'. I want you boys to be there. Ain't nobody but you boys allowed below on *Muskrat.* "

Hoyt Crane and John Dryden took a deep breath. This means that they would get their money back.

"Boys, you listen real good to what I'm about to say."

The meeting was deadly serious. You could hear a pin drop.

"Tonight your goin' to learn some things ain't no one else knows 'cept John Allen, my yard crew and me. When you come over to the shed and see *Muskrat*, you're goin' to know the secret. Ain't no way you can sail this boat and not know.

"If a millionth of an inch of anybody in this room thinks he has to tell his wife or son or best friend or anybody 'bout the *Muskrat*, git out of here right now. You can't tell nobody.

"If she's as fast as I think she might be and the competition finds out why, it ain't too late for them to do the same thing we done. Anybody in this room not understand?"

Nick asked each crew member, "Hoyt?"

"I'd never tell the secret, Nick."

"Hambden Martin?"

"No sir. Never!."

"Allison Deemer?"

"No, sir."

"Glenn Parrot?"

"Never."

"Bailey Shultz?"

"Never."

"Peter Dillon?"

"Not a chance, sir."

"Bradley Brown?"

"No way."

"Drake Cochran?"

"I don't know no secret. How can I tell it if I don't know it?"

"Damn it, Drake! You're goin' to know tonight when you see the boat you dumb ass!"

"Oh.... Ah no, I ain't tellin' nobody. I won't even tell my cat."

"Mark Litty?"

"No."

"Herbert Loscomb"?

"No sir."

"Schuyler Mattingly?"

"Not on your life. I want that cup!"

"Jimmy Firth?"

"I'm with Schuyler."

"Vaughn Downes?"

"No sir. Sam here's got too much money tied up to say anything." Everybody chuckled.

Nick felt his secret was safe with the *Muskrat* crew. He and Sam had arranged for security during the next several months including aboard the ship.

Nick summed up what he had to say, "Boys, Mr. Johnson, I think the *Muskrat* will be the fastest boat I've ever built. She should foot with anybody on the wind and she'll out point 'em. Reachin' and running, ain't neither boat built will touch her.

Keep in mind, the America's Cup Course has been revised this time. There's more down wind legs, and that's where we should eat them up. You got a fine boat to take to Australia. Good luck to you. I'll see you at my yard at midnight tonight."

After a loud round of applause, Sam stood again. "Well that's it boys. If anybody forgets their promise about the secret, you better do it on your way out of town and you'd better have some speed on.

"I'll see you at midnight."

The meeting broke up at around nine o'clock, and the boys wandered down to Dryden's.

They sat at a corner table overlooking the creek and Ralph's Boatyard. They couldn't wait to see her.

At midnight, the boys got in their cars and arrived at Ralph's Boatyard. Nick and Sam met them at the gate. John Allen was on the boat working on some finishing touches. Nick clapped his hands to quiet the geese down.

"Well boys. You're about to see the fastest twelve ever to hit the water. Ready?"

The boys were more than ready.

"John Allen and I slid her over a little while ago. She's layin' in the railway slip. Come look her over boys."

Everyone was so excited. They were finally going to see the *Muskrat*. They went down the side of the shed, and as they turned the corner, she came into view. There, glistening under the floodlights, was the yacht *Muskrat*."

She was utterly magnificent; painted a navy blue with a bold red and white boot top. Her decks were robin egg blue with a ten inch strip of white separating it from the hull. Along each side, there were twenty five blue and red stars running along the white stripe. Halfway down the stripe, there was a break and the name *Muskrat* in bold, gold script. The name was edged in red and white. On the transom, again in gold, were the letters U.S.A. Just under that, was the Tred Avon Yacht Club burgee and under the burgee in small gold letters, was Oxford, Maryland. Tom Norton had done the fancy paint job, and it was done to perfection.

Her decks were as clean as a snow covered field. There were no coffee grinders cluttering them up, only the drums and a few smaller winches.

An unusual feature was her helmsman's cockpit. It was positioned just aft of the mast and there were two wheels. Aft of the helm was a larger cockpit where the crew could reach the winches and the two large barrels. From there, Bailey had a good view of the sail for trimming. Allison would trim the main from this position and Hambden Martin, the tactician, would be stationed there also. On each side of the spar, was a small deck opening in the shape of a rectangle running fore and aft. Three men could fit into one of these openings. There were some other unusual features. For instance, the traveler was all the way aft. On the foredeck, there were two hatches, each about two and one half feet wide and about fifteen feet long. The deck layout was unusual to say the least.

Everyone was more than impressed. They were flabbergasted, amazed, and astounded at what Nick had done. Even though they weren't privy to the reasoning behind the layout, they were impressed by it.

Sam was the first to go below. Hoyt was right behind him. Neither man said a word. They simply studied what was before them, looked at each other, and smiled. It sure made sense. Soon the entire crew had gathered below. It was so simple. Why hadn't anyone else thought of it?

Old Man Nick Benson stood at the small companionway and listened to the comments. He was very proud of the

Muskrat. He didn't think of it as his creation though. This racing machine was the culmination of four generations of hard work. It had started with his grandfather Ralph and the *Maggie P.* "I wish Ralph could be here." he thought to himself.Nick sat down in the companionway looking down at Sam and the crew. His feet were on the small ladder leading below.

"Well, Sam, what do you think?"

"Nick, it's ingenious; the secret, that is. Are you sure it's legal?"

"It's legal, Sam. We'll know for sure tomorrow. The boat will be officially measured." Nick didn't seem too worried.

"How about the secret? Will they reveal the secret?"

"No, Sam, they didn't reveal the Aussie secret did they?"

"I guess your right. That wouldn't be fair. Nick, I understand the secret. That's so obvious I can't believe it. There are some other things I don't understand, like that contraption there."

Sam pointed to what looked like a very complicated apparatus sitting on the bottom of the hull. It consisted of four seats that slid back and forth on tracks. It looked like Nick had taken the guts out of four rowing shells and placed them below; two facing the other two. On either side of each seat was the handle end of an oar.

Nick explained the machine, "I seen these people out in the creek in these shells, Sam. I was amazed at the power they could generate. Well, one day John Allen was out getting a cripple. He was rowing his heart out. Now keep in mind, John Allen ain't no sissy rower. This old woman come along and passed him in that shell like he was tied. That got me to thinkin'. What I come up with, is what you see right there. By four men rowing that machine, there is a heap of power. As you can see, it turns that large chain like a bicycle chain, and that chain is connected to the large drums on deck. It can also be switched to any halyards on the boat. The man in the cockpit just decides which gear to put it in and that's it.

"It made a lot of sense. A man rowing uses his arms and legs, not just his arms like on a coffee grinder. The power you could generate from four men would be unbelievable. It would triple the power of a grinder.

"We will murder anybody who gets into a tacking duel boys. Them grinders can't do what we can. Can't come close. Our sails will go up like a flash and come in like a flash."

Nick was a genius. He explained further, "Now you know why I wanted the grinders to practice in the shells. Now, boys, I want to tell you something real serious. I keep sayin' that this America's Cup ain't goin' to be like the rest. It ain't Newport. I've studied it real hard, like I done them shells. Five months of racin' down there is gonna wear down most of the men. I ain't kiddin' ya. Remember, shorter legs; more of 'em and heavy winds and seas. It's gonna be a killer boys. You'd better be in shape. You can bet your ass your boat will be. She ain't gonna break and you better not either.

"I've designed the *Muskrat* for the Indian Ocean, not Newport or the Chesapeake Bay. Let me tell you 'bout some things just between us.

"Remember, ain't nodody knows nothing about *Muskrat* 'cept us. To the rest of the world, we're a bunch of Eastern Shoremen that are just as dumb as clams. Let's keep it that way. It's what they call low profile.

"Now you seen the cockpit. All the other boats will have their cockpit all the way aft. It don't make sense. Shee-it! Sparklin and Stepens will spend a half-a-million dollars trying to keep the weight out of the bow and stern of a boat. So what do they do? They put the boat in the water and down the dock comes a three hundred pound helmsman and where the hell does he sit his fat ass for the day, right in the stern of the gawd damn boat. Now if that makes sense then a goose don't honk and a crab don't bite. You got to keep the weight out of the ends of the boat. Shee-it, anybody knows that!

"Now here's somethin' else I ain't never told. The wood that the bow and stern are made of on all my boats ain't the same as the wood in the middle. The wood in the ends is called ruddynut. You ain't never heard of ruddynut, and I'll tell you why. As far as I know, there's only one stand of it on the shore. Maybe the only stand anywhere. It's down to lower Darchester. My grandaddy found it when he was duck shootin' down there and bought all three hundred acres. Ain't neither kind a wood like it. It's strong as oak and weighs 'bout the same as balsa. The ends of the Muskrat is made out of ruddynut; and if you don't think that ain't gonna help in them heavy seas down there, you're dead wrong. You'll see. Them boats with ends too heavy gonna to be the same as ridin' a bucking bronco. She'll hobby horse you to death, cap'n. You can bank on it.

"Now, when we get to the Oxford Boatyard, you'll find out somethin' else. The boom on *Muskrat* is about eight feet longer than any you've ever seen on a twelve meter. She'll look like the boom on the *Maggie P*. We can git away with that because of the secret. Now, what that does is this: I ain't gonna help on the wind, but it ain't gonna hurt. Remember there's an extra leg this time. It's a running leg, boys, and that's where we git 'em. Ain't neither boat gonna reach or run with *Muskrat* .

"Now, I keep talkin' 'bout high winds. The higher the wind the more the boat heels. If they heel enough, the foot of the jib's in the water. You mark my word, they'll be more than one jib torn up by water rippin' the skirt. They'll be big seas rollin' over the weather bow. Them jibs can't take it. They're gonna blow out. Plus, the boat blocks the wind from it. We ain't gonna have that problem on here. All our jibs is cut so the clew is about ten feet off the deck. That keeps it out of the water and in the wind. It's the same size, but it's better. When a wave rolls over *Muskrat's* bow, it ain't gonna hit the jib. It'll hit the water cause our jibs is all high cut. Besides that, Hoyt will be steerin' just behind the mast. The high cut jib will let him see good. He's in the middle of the boat so he can judge things better from there, too.

"Now the two rectangular openings on either side of the spar are for the foredeck crew. They're little pockets where the boys can git in when they ain't busy. No sense in hangin' on the weather rail, ridin' a buckin' bronco, drinkin' salt water and bein' miserable. When there ain't nothin' to do, they can be to weather and out of the wind. Won't be neither person on deck. Remember those two long hatches on the foredeck? That's where you store your headsails. They won't wash overboard and you always have two ready to go. Just flip open a hatch and the boys below get to grindin' and it's up. It's gonna be real important. It's gonna save a lot of sails bein' overboard when we're changin'."

Samuel E. Johnson, III and the crew were so excited they couldn't stand it. The secret was ingenious, yet simple. No boat builder anywhere in the world had thought of it. To top it off, old man Nick had improved nearly every single inch of the twelve. The man was a genius. It all made so much sense, it just had to work.

"When the world sees this machine, it'll make every other racin' boat obsolete," Hoyt thought to himself.

Under the cover of darkness, they towed the *Muskrat* over to the Oxford Boatyard. There were two men waiting for them to help with the spars. They were not allowed onboard, however, just the *Muskrat* crew and John Dryden would be allowed below for some time.

The spar went in nicely with no problems at all. The rigging was not unusual except for the permanent backstay. Nick had designed a backstay arrangement that was different than any other they had ever seen. To accommodate the extra long boom, the backstay was attached to the very tip of the reversed transom. Attached to the forward end of the transom was a double strut that extended at a forty-five degree angle toward the aft end. It was about fifteen feet long and could be eased hydraulically or tightened. This allowed room for the long boom and extra mainsail. For the backstay to have the same angle without the strut, the boat would have to be another ten feet long. Old man Nick was pretty slick.

The boys had the boat rigged by three o'clock. They then towed her to the ferry dock at the foot of Morris Street, the main street in Oxford.

Sam Johnson drove Nick home. He paid him his bonus for finishing early and gave him another check for $75,000.

"Nick, give each of your yard crew five grand and you and John Allen divide up the rest." Nick was very appreciative.

"Nick, if the *Muskrat* doesn't ever win a race, I think her builder thought more and worked harder on her than any other twelve ever built. I'll always think that, Nick. You have done a wonderful job."

"Gawd damn, Sam! If that bucket don't ever win neither race, I'm gonna throw a pair of oars over my shoulder and start walkin' inland. When I git far enough to where somebody asks me what them wooden things are I'm totin', I'm gonna settle down there and start a raisin' banny roosters. It'll be no more boat buildin' for me."

The crew secured the *Muskrat* and it was decided that Jimmy Firth would stay aboard until six a.m., when Schuyler would relieve him.

The companionway openings each had doors that could be locked in place when the boat was not racing. These would be stowed on the *Oxford Queen* when not in use.

John invited the crew to his bar for a beer before they all hit the rack for the night. What a night it had been. They were so excited they wouldn't sleep anyway. They went to the cooler, grabbed a longneck, and gathered at their usual corner table.

"I'm so excited 'bout that boat, I can't stand it." Hoyt was like a little kid on Christmas morning.

"I ain't!"

"What the hell's your problem Drake?"

"Mostly the paint job. All them stars and fancy gold names an' all. Geese should be comin' soon. Should a painted her camouflage and shot outta her 'til she shipped out. Gawd damn, she'd hold ten guns I'll bet."

"Camouflage! That's the dumbest idea you've had yet, Drake! Well, one of 'em anyway." Hoyt couldn't believe it.

John thought Nick's invention was great. "That's the damnest way I ever seen to trim sails, Hoyt."

"You got that right, John. It makes sense to me. I can't believe Nick figured that out. The man's a genius. Do you know how fast we can tack that boat? It'll be the first time I ever looked forward to a tackin' duel."

Bradley Brown was impressed too. He thought it would save a lot of energy as opposed to a coffee grinder.

Drake was not as happy about it. "Gawd damn if I think its so great! I could spend five months racin' a twelve meter and never see the sun or another boat!"

"Don't worry, Drake. We'll take a picture of all the other

twelves and tape the one we're racin' against to one of your oars!" Hoyt said kiddingly.

"Yeah, Nick's got some brown paint over at the yard for your tan, Drake." Hambden joined in the fun.

"Hoyt, do you like the helm so far forward?"

"Bradley, getting the weight out of the stern makes sense. I ain't sure I'll be able to handle her in a jibe as good. Can't see the main as well. Other than that it's O.K. I'll be able to read the jib better. I sure in hell got to remember I got almost forty feet of boat behind me when things get tight. I'm liable to be sailing a six meter and Allison trimming the main on another one if I do forgit."

Drake didn't agree as usual. "Dumbest place I ever seen to steer from. It ain't no Greyhound bus. Next thing you know, Nick will move the cockpit to the first spreaders, so Hoyt can see good!"

"Oh shut up, Drake!"

Hambden Martin had another thought. "You remember when Nick said it wouldn't hurt with the luffing rule to have the cockpit forward? I've been thinking about that, and you know, he's right." Hambden was the tactician for the *Muskrat*. It would be he who would tell Hoyt when to tack and when to jibe. He would time and call the starts. He knew every rule in the book backwards and forwards. He was very good.

He explained, "Rule 38.2 says the boat to leeward can't luff ya if the regular helm station of the boat to weather's abeam or forward of the other boat's mast. That means the further forward the wheel is, the less a boat can luff you. We can luff the other boat twice as much as they can us. That gawd damn Nick's somethin'. Ain't neither barnacle on that boy's bottom!"

"Hambden, you're right as rain." Hoyt was impressed once again. "That could mean the difference in a tight race. What

74

did you boys think of the hatches on the foredeck?"

Schuyler Mattingly thought they made a lot of sense. "Ya know Hoyt, Nick keeps talkin' about lots of wind and heavy seas. If he's right, them sail lockers are gonna be real handy. I studied them right close. Now think about it. If it's blowin' nineteen knots before the race and it's between the heavy number one and number two, you can go with the number one. You can put the number two in one locker ready to go. Depending on what the forecast is, you can put the number three or light number one in the other one. You got three headsails ready to go up in a second. Ain't gotta send three men below draggin' up another sail. If you want to change clothes, you open a locker, hoist her up, and drop the first jib into the same locker. Make's sense to me."

"I'll tell ya something else, Schuyler."

"Not 'till I get another longneck, Vaughn."

Schuyler got another round for everybody and sat back down.

Vaughn continued, "I've done a lot of ocean racin' and I'll tell you boys somethin'. One of the things that will git you into trouble when it breezes up is getting a jib overboard. I've seen jibs tied down on the foredeck been washed half overboard by the ties rippin' in the seas. A big wave packs some power, I'll tell ya. It's like a swan rappin' ya in the nose. If he keeps it up long enough, that nose is gonna break. Remember, ain't no life lines on no twelve. I think them sail lockers gonna save us a heap a trouble."

Drake broke in, "I think those lockers are good myself. You can get two people in one up to seven foot tall. After this racin', we can bring her back to the Chesapeake, paint her black, and use her as a marine hearse."

"Aw shut up, Drake!"

"You know, I like them little foredeck cockpits too. You can git below out ot the wind and still be to weather. I bet you can catch your breath better then tryin' to hang on the rail. Foredeck works gonna be a bear sound's like. We'll need all the help we can git."

Allison Deemer piped up, "Those high cut headsails make a world of sense to me. I've seen some jibs that have a cringle half way up the foot. When the boat heeled, they'd put a halyard in the cringle and raise the foot out of the water. A higher cut foot is a much better idea."

"Sounds like you got a lot a main to deal with, Allison, with that long boom and all. Do you think you can handle it all right? I'll bet Hoyt will be callin' for ease a lot and then want it right back." Hambden was a little concerned. It would be a huge mainsail for Allison to handle.

Allison wasn't worried in the least. "The vang is hydraulic and the mainsail trim can be geared over to the rowers below. I would guess those boys could pull the spar down if you let'em." She was right.

Thank God Nick spotted those shells in the creek. A system like that wasn't needed on the bay or even in Newport, but it was perfect for where they were heading.

"That ruddynut wood must be worth a fortune. I'd like to git some of them seeds and grow a few." Pete Dillon said.

"It's hard to believe them Bensons kept that secret for all these years . Speakin' of that, what do you all think about the secret?"

"I ain't so sure it's legal, John. But if it is, I think it'll work."

Hoyt Crane would feel a lot better after the boat was measured. What a blow it would be if after all this we are declared illegal. They would know in a few hours.

"Let me ask you something boys. If the *Maggie P.* had the

76

same secret as the *Muskrat*, how come nobody that sailed on her knew what it was." Allison had a good point.

"It weren't the same, Allison." John explained, "What Nick done was take the idea from the *Maggie P.*, but he, what you call, developed it into what's in the *Muskrat*. Nick explained it all to me. The way it works is the same, but the way it looks ain't. Ain't nobody could figure it out back then cause it looked different."

"I see. Then no one would know what the secret was. Now I understand." Allison was satisfied.

"Bet it ain't legal." Drake said.

"Why ain't it, Einstein? I'm sure you can explain to Hoyt and all of us why it ain't. You want me to git your slide rule for you?"

John was getting a little annoyed.

Glenn Parrott spoke up, "Only slide rule Drake ever knowed was on a log canoe. The rule that says when you slide your ass out on the hikin' board, you slide to weather."

Everybody broke up laughing; everybody except Drake that is.

"Drake, is there anything about the *Muskrat* and our trip to Australia you're happy about?" John was still a little peeved.

"Yeah, I'm gawd damn glad we're goin' to be racin' in January and February."

"Why's that, you tared of tongin'?"

"Ain't that. But if I've got to spend five months sittin' below on a sailboat, rowin' a gawd damn seat back and forth, I'm glad it's gonna be in the winter. Least it'll be nice and cold. Will they race in snowstorms? Gawd damn, I never thought about that. We don't want to forget our snow shovels."

"Gawd damn it, Drake, there ain't gonna be no snow-storms. It's summer in Australia when it's our winter, you dumb ass. It's gonna be hot down there." John was on edge again.

"You mean to tell me, startin' October fifth, I climb down inside the *Muskrat* when it's hotter than hell, and row a damn bicycle chain around and around for five months includin' Christmas, and the only thing I got to look at is Bradley sittin' across from me, rowin' his seat? How would you like to look at Bradley for five months? I'll tell you one good thing 'bout Bradley. I'm damn glad he's alive, 'cause if he wasn't, I'd be the ugliest man in Oxford."

Bradley jumped out of his chair, dove across the table, and grabbed Drake by his shirt. Longnecks went everywhere, crashing into bits and pieces as they hit the floor.

"You son of a bitch, Drake! I'm gonna kill you! Don't you worry 'bout where you gonna be Christmas. Only thing you'll want for Christmas is your doctor. When I'm finished with you, you won't know where you are, let alone where Australia is. Ain't no heat problem where I'm gonna send you boy!"

They were tossing around on the floor, each with a tight grip on the other. They were two big men. Luckily, they never threw any punches.

John, Mark Litty and Herbert, with some help from the others, got them apart before any damage was done.

"All right, gang; that's it! It's late. Let's get some sleep!" Drake and Bradley shook hands. John bid everybody good night, cleaned up the mess, and hit the rack.

Everybody went home to get some sleep. The men were coming to measure the boat on Monday and they all wanted to be there.

Schuyler Mattingly didn't go home. It was almost six o'clock. He wandered down to the *Muskrat* to relieve Jimmy .

Chapter Four

Soon things were buzzing at Brinkley's. "Have you been down to the ferry dock? Have you seen her?"

The *Muskrat* was all anybody talked about. At about nine o'clock, there were sixteen people on the dock looking her over.

"Oh come on, Schuyler. Let me on. Shee-it! I ain't gonna tell nobody 'bout no secret."

Walter the town cop stepped in. "Anybody steps one foot on that boat, I'll arrest you. Strict orders from the town commisioners. No exceptions. You hear me?"

"Yes sir!" said Freddie Randall in a real smart tone. Freddie was the town troublemaker. "I'll get on that damn boat," he thought to himself. "I'll know every inch of her bottom before the day's out." He figured he'd get under the wharf up by the shore and wade out. When he got to deeper water, the wharf would hide him as he swam to the *Muskrat*. Then he'd simply dive down and take a look. He went home to get his swimsuit.

God knows what Freddie would do if he found something he wasn't supposed to find. He had been in and out of jail four times, and he was only nineteen. Wouldn't it be a shame if the Benson secret got out before the races by a young thug like Freddie.

People came down to the dock all morning. There must have been two hundred visitors by ten-thirty, and the crowds grew as the word spread. Everyone thought she was gorgeous.

There was a small poster tacked to the dock in front of *Muskrat* that read:

Saturday 10:00 *Muskrat* **Parade**
Noon Christening • 2:00 Crab Feast
Street Dance Following
For All the People of Oxford

What a nice thing for Sam to do. He invited the entire town to christen the boat and treat them to a crab feast and dance. *Muskrat* really was to be the pride of Oxford.

At noon, the dock was filled with admirers. Two gentlemen dressed in white pants and blue blazers appeared. They looked spiffy, sporting their black and red bowties, white shoes; each wearing a white captain's hat.

With them were two younger men dressed in white pants and blue polo shirts. They were official measurers from the Royal Perth Yacht Club, arriving at twelve o'clock on the dot.

The entire crew of the *Muskrat* had returned to the dock and was enjoying conversations with fellow townspeople. Nick and Sam Johnson were just coming down the hill toward the ferry dock as the men approached.

"Sir, we are from the Royal Perth Yacht Club and are here to measure this yacht. We would like permission to come aboard."

"Ain't neither person can git on this boat without Samuel E. Johnson, III sayin' they can." Schuyler would't allow them to get on.

"But, sir, you don't understand. We're from Australia."

"I don't care if you're angels from heaven, gawd damn it. You ain't gittin' aboard this here boat."

"It's okay Schuyler." Sam spoke up as he and Nick reached the end of the dock.

"Allow me to introduce myself. I'm Samuel E. Johnson III

and this is Mr. Nick Benson. My friend on the *Muskrat* is Schuyler Mattingly. He was just following orders."

"I'm Sir Oswald Timly and this is Mr. Mathew Oslo. We are the official measurers. We are here to oversee these men in measuring your yacht."

"Please come aboard." Sam gestured toward the *Muskrat*.

Sir Oswald and his crew took their jobs very seriously, never cracking a smile.

Drake was standing on the dock next to John Dryden. They were very interested in what was taking place aboard the *Muskrat*. Drake punched John in the ribs with his elbow.

"Sir Waldo and his boys would be good when we git back on the marine hearse, John. They got all the looks of undertakers."

"Shhh, they may hear you, Drake!"

Sir Oswald Timly and his men went over the *Muskrat* with a fine tooth comb. They measured everything from the length of the boom and mast to the height of the toe rail.

When Sir Oswald first went below, he looked around very carefully. He glanced at Sam, and then rolled his eyes. This scared Sam to death.

"Ah, anything wrong, Sir Oswald?" Sir Oswald simply took a deep breath and continued with his notes. At the end of three-and-one-half hours, Sir Oswald punched all the information he had into a computer, and then approached Sam, who was standing by a shroud.

"Mr. Johnson. I have completed our measurement. I bid you good day, sir."

"But Sir Oswald, tell me please! Is there anything on this boat that is in your opinion unusual or, I mean, illegal?" Sam couldn't wait any longer. His nerves were on edge and his patience was shot. There was complete silence. The entire crew was at the end of the dock waiting for his reply. Old man Nick got a little closer so he could hear.

All of a sudden, there was this ear bursting shrieking sound coming from where Sir Oswald and Sam were standing. It sounded like someone in excruciating pain. Someone was yelling at the top of his voice.

"What the hell is that, Drake?" John asked.

It seemed to be coming from below the dock. Drake looked down and spotted Freddie Randall thrashing and shrieking in the water between *Muskrat* and the wharf. John got down on his knees, reached out, and yanked Freddie out of the water. Freddie had followed through with his plan to find out the secret of the *Muskrat*. There was only one problem. Surrounding the boat was a thin metal net through which thousands of volts of electricity passed. Freddy had found the net.

Everyone settled down and Sam questioned Sir Oswald again. "Well, Sir Oswald, what is your answer?"

"The answer to your question, Mr. Johnson, is yes."

Nick couldn't believe it, Sam's heart jumped. The boys on the dock were taken aback.

Nick Benson stepped forward, "You mean she's illegal, Sir Oswald?"

"I didn't say she is illegal, Mr Benson. She is within the measuring rules. She's a twelve meter. What I said was she is unusual. She's the most unusual twelve I've ever measured. As a matter of fact, she's the most unusual boat I've ever been on. Good day sir."

Everybody on the dock went beserk. "Hooray! Hooray! Yea *Muskrat* ! She's a twelve! She's a twelve!"

Sam nearly fainted. Nick was relieved to say the least.

"I told you she was legal, Sam."

"Thank Christ she is, Nick. I was about ready to ask for my

money back."

It was nine-thirty in the morning, and the manager of the Oxford little league team, Epps Hickman, was getting his boys lined up for the big parade. The kids were excited. After the parade, they would see the christening of *Muskrat* and then they'd be treated to a wonderful crab feast. If that wasn't enough, a street dance would bring the day to a close.

At ten-fifteen, the people were lined up at the town park. They could see the parade making the turn at the causeway and coming towards them up Morris Street. Everyone turned out to see. From nearly every house flew the American flag. The entire town was very much into what was taking place. The Easton High School Band was leading the parade. Easton is a larger town located about ten miles from Oxford. The Oxford children go to school at Easton High.

Little Jason Wyatt was jumping up and down in his excitement. Jason was six years old, and his favorite thing in the whole wide world was a parade. As the band passed by, little Jason marched in place. He couldn't wait until he was old enough to participate.

Following the band were the three Town Commissioners. They rode in a beautiful 1942 Rolls Royce which belonged to Judge John C. Southard. The Judge collected antique cars and had two in the parade. As he drove down Morris Street, it was evident he was enjoying showing off his car.

Behind the commissioners was the largest of Oxford's three fire trucks. The sound of its engine was deafening as it passed with its many lights blinking before the crowd. Jason stood in awe as the fire truck passed by. Following the truck came the fire company members in their dress uniforms, led by the flag bearer proudly carrying the American flag. There were eighteen firemen marching in the parade.

The fire company was followed by a flatbed truck sponsored by the Brinsfield Crab House. Brinsfield's was the largest of three crab houses in Oxford. The crabbers sold their catch to these houses. Each house employed several crab pickers who extracted the delicious meat from its shell.

On the truck was a large wooden picnic table. Seated at the table, facing the back of the flatbed, was Miss Nattie Green. Miss Nattie was the champion crab picker of Talbot County. Every year, Brinsfield's sponsored a crab picking contest, and every year, Miss Nattie won. Jason watched as the flatbed truck passed by.

After Brinsfield's Crab House came a horse and buggy owned by a nearby farmer. He and his wife were dressed in costumes typical of the Eighteen Hundreds.

Jason was a little puzzled by the next group in the parade. It looked like a marching band, but no one had their instruments.

"Where's the horns and drums, Daddy?" Jason asked his father.

"That's not a band, son. It's the crew of the *Muskrat* . The new boat we saw at the ferry dock. They're the whole reason for the parade . It's a celebration for the new twelve meter from Oxford, Jason."

The crowd got real excited when the boys came by and gave them a wonderful round of applause. To think they were going halfway around the world to try to bring back The America's Cup was almost too much to believe.

The boys were all decked out in white ducks and blue blazers. Samuel E. Johnson, III had bought each of them a spiffy uniform. On the pocket of each blazer was a handsome patch. It was rather large and round and had a black background. In the middle was a design with a shape similar to a policeman's badge. The top of the badge was blue and the lower two thirds was done in red and white vertical stripes. Around the insignia, in handsome gold letters was written: America's Cup 1987. In the middle of the insignia was written: U. S. 50--the sail number of the *Muskrat* .

Drake felt very uncomfortable marching in the parade. He was next to Vaughn Downes.

"Everybody's lookin' at us, Vaughn."

"No shit, Drake! We're in a parade!"

"I hate these dumb uniforms. I guess they put U.S. 50 on our coats in case we get lost. U.S. Route 50 goes right through Easton."

"Damn it Drake, it ain't a road, it's the sail number of *Muskrat*! It's the fiftieth twelve meter that the United States has entered in the America's Cup."

"Oh. Ya know, Vaughn, there's only one thing I can think of that's worse than marching in a parade."

Vaughn took a deep breath, wondering what Drake would come up with next. "What's worse than marchin' in a parade, Drake?"

"What's worse than marching in a parade, is marching in a parade behind a horse, and here we are, right behind the only horse in the whole parade. Better watch where you step Vaughn. I'll be glad when this is over."

Behind the crew, in the other antique car belonging to Judge Southard, were old man Nick Benson and Samuel E. Johnson, III with their wives. They, too, got a round of applause. Nick and Sam were very proud.

Following them was the Oxford Community Center Float. Mrs. Stanford, who ran the Oxford Day Camp for the local children, had organized the building of the float. The children had made a huge replica of the America's Cup out of chicken wire and aluminum foil. The cup stood about eight feet tall. The handle of the cup was made out of two bicycle handle bars and was attached to a six-by-six post running down the middle of the cup and screwed to the wooden floor of the float. The handle was very strong.

Mrs. Stanford and the children had made a very elaborate kangaroo costume, which was worn by Betsy Fountain. They had also made a costume that looked like a muskrat. Little Tucker Fountain, Betsy's younger brother, wore the muskrat costume. As the float traveled down Morris Street, the muskrat and kangaroo pulled and tugged on the cup, seemingly trying to wrestle the cup from the other. It was little Jason's favorite part of the parade.

After the float came another fire truck on which rode the Oxford Fire Queen for 1986, Mandy Hollowell, who had just turned sixteen.

The last parade entry was sponsored by the Creek Restaurant, which was located close to Dryden's Bar. A huge banner about six feet high and ten feet wide was held up by ten-foot poles on each end of the banner. Two waiters from the Creek Restaurant carried the poles; Craig Detling and Doug Banks. The banner appeared at a rather severe angle since Doug was much taller than Craig. The banner simply said: "Go *Muskrat!*"

Young Jason was disappointed that the parade was over, but there were many more activities to enjoy this day.

Everyone followed the parade down to the ferry dock. There the crowd gathered at the end of the wharf. The *Muskrat* was elegant. Sam made sure his ensign was oversized. That was one thing he loved to see, a large ensign on a boat. It drove him crazy to see tiny little flags on boats, flown by people who didn't know any better. The Tred Avon Yacht Club burgee was flying from the spar. The boys had eased the stern lines and tightened the bow, so Mrs. Johnson could reach the stem with a bottle of champagne. She would have the honor of christening the boat.

The ceremony was very brief. First the President of the Town Commissioners spoke: "I know I speak for the entire town when I say we are very proud to be a part of this yacht and the task she is about to attempt. Even though we will not be boarding that airplane as you will the fifteenth, we all will be with you the entire way. Our thoughts and our prayers go with you. Good luck, and God bless the *Muskrat*."

Hoyt Crane asked Sam if he could say a word. "I ain't much on speeches," he said, "but I want to say somethin' for the *Muskrat* crew.

"We sure appreciate Mr. Johnson giving us this chance to show that us Eastern Shoremen can pack with the best. We're grateful to Nick Benson and John Allen for all their work and especially for Nick's ideas 'bout boats." Hoyt became very emotional and his voice began to tremble.

"This whole town came out today for us and we ain't never gonna forget that." A tear ran down Hoyt's cheek.

"Ain't nobody knows what's gonna happen to us and the *Muskrat* . We're up against the best in the world. But I can promise you this: Ain't neither boat gonna whip us cause we didn't give it our best. Them other boys got a fight on their hands, I can promise you that." Another tear rolled down Hoyt's cheek.

"Thanks again for bein' here today. We'll never forgit it." The crowd responded with a thunderous applause.

Mrs. Sam Johnson stood and said, "I christen thee *Muskra!*" and after a generous backswing, cracked the bottle of champagne on the stem of *Muskrat* .

"To the *Muskrat* !" someone in the crew yelled.

Everybody joined in: "Hip hip hooray! Hip hip hooray. Hip hip hooray!"

It was a very moving ceremony. The crew, Nick and Mr. Johnson were all very touched by the sincerity of the town's people, and they in turn were touched to have been included. The *Muskrat* was truly a bond that held everyone closely together. Even those who had been unfriendly neighbors to each other put hostile thoughts aside for that moment. It was a very special day for Oxford and the *Muskrat* .

The crowd enjoyed the steamed crabs and cold beer all afternoon. Sam had the Creek Restaurant cater the affair. It was a real Eastern Shore celebration. It was like one big happy family. No one had his nose in the air at this party. Fifty tables had been set up and on each one there was a big pile of steamed crabs in the middle. On either side of the pile of crabs was a large plate of steaming hot corn on the cob, and next to that dish was a plate of large red sliced tomatoes. Smaller plates of pickles and cheese rounded out the menu.

Bill Bateman who owned Plimhimmon Farm provided the corn and tomatoes which Bill's son-in-law, Terry, had spent the entire day before picking. He had a special interest in the *Muskrat* . He was commodore of the Tred Avon Yacht Club whose burgee the *Muskrat* would fly.

Two beer trucks parked on either end of the eating area. Before the night was over, twenty-one kegs would be empty in addition to the soft drinks that were served.

Everyone had their fill of crabs, and at about seven-thirty, the dock band started. The townspeople danced till one a.m. and could have gone all night.

Samuel E. Johnson, III had done himself and the *Muskrat* proud. The day had been one of Oxford's finest and would never be forgotten.

Chapter Five

The following Thursday, the spar was removed from *Muskrat* and the *Oxford Queen* towed her to Baltimore. They would be shipped to Australia, leaving the next day. Unfortunately there wasn't any time to do any sailing aboard the twelve. The *Oxford Queen* was loaded with extra rigging, spars, sails, and just about anything you could imagine including several hundred cases of Budweiser longnecks.

The next time the boys would see the *Muskrat*, she would be in the Indian Ocean.

Sam Johnson, John Dryden and the crew stepped aboard a 747, and at nine in the morning took off for San Francisco. After a brief stop in Honolulu, they landed in Sydney, Australia at seven thirty a.m. the next day. Everyone was exhausted. As they were getting off the plane, Drake was standing next to Sam.

"Gawd damn glad we're finally here. I thought for a while the pilot couldn't find Australia and was makin' another loop."

Sam smiled. "It's a long flight all right Drake."

"Is our hotel far from here? I can't wait to get some sleep."

"Drake, our hotel is almost three thousand miles from here. We're in Sydney. Our hotel is in Perth, on the western end of Australia."

"I knew damn well he was lost. I knew it."

Upon boarding their plane to Perth, Schuyler read to

Bradley from the travel brochure Pucky Lappen had given him.

"Australia is a large country indeed. It is about the same size as the continental United States and is considered either the smallest continent in the world or the largest island. It is the only continent inhabited by a single nation.

"Australia is made up of six states and two territories. The largest state is Western Australia which is four times the size of Texas. Perth and Fremantle are located in this state where the cup races will take place. The other states are South Australia, New South Wales,where Sydney is located, Victoria, and Tasmania.

"The Australians or 'Aussies' as they are called are easy to live with. They are very hospitable and very down-to-earth. It matters not how wealthy or from what social background you come. It is from your heart you are judged in the land down under.

"Aussies love a good time and are noted to have more than their share of 'Tinnies'(cans of beer) at the local pub each afternoon.

"They are also noted for their unusual accent. Even though their language is English, it sounds more like Swahili at times.

"Besides, the unusual accent, Aussies are famous the world over for their slang.

"Chuck a willy' means go berserk.

'My shout' is 'my round' in a bar.

'A 'Wowser' is a prude.

'Don't get off your bike' means calm down.

'Oz' is Australian and 'Freo' is Fremantel.

'G'day' means Good day.

"At times, it is virtually impossible to determine what an Aussie is saying."

Schuyler's dissertation was interrupted by the sound of

snoring. As Sky took his eyes from the brochure and looked up, he discovered Bradley in a sound sleep.

After a five hour flight, the crew of the *Muskrat* landed in Perth at six-thirty in the evening. Their trip consisted of twenty-six hours in the air.

They gathered their baggage and hired cabs to take them to their hotel. They would stay in Perth until the boats arrived. Sam, Drake, John and Hoyt got in the first cab. "Meet you boys at the hotel," Sam said as they were driving off.

Sam gave the driver instructions. "We would like to go to the Merlin Hotel, please."

The driver nodded and snapped everyone's head back as he took off as if in the Indy 500. He raced out of the airport.

Drake was sitting in the front seat, his eyes big as saucers. The taxi was racing down Mill Street in heavy traffic and Drake spotted a large truck heading for them.

"Damn it, you're gonna kill us!" Drake yelled at the driver.

"Drake! Settle down!" John yelled from the back seat. Everyone was tired and a little edgy.

"I didn't come all the way over here to git killed. Git over driver. Damn, git over to your side of the road!"

"He's chucked a willey! " the driver yelled at Drake. Of course, Drake didn't understand.

"This som'bitch is drunk as a monkey! Give me that wheel!" Drake grabbed the steering wheel with both hands. By this time, John Dryden had leaned over the seat and grabbed Drake's arms trying to pry them from the steering wheel.

"Git over! Gawd damn, you're on the wrong side of the road."

Three men wrestling one wheel was too much. The steering wheel snapped and there they were; John, Drake, and the driver hanging on to an unattached steering wheel doing about forty down a busy street in Perth. The car drifted left and hit a light pole, snapping it off at the base. The top of the pole landed on the opposite side of the street forming a closed gate for the rest of the traffic. Upon hitting the pole, the car flipped on its left side and turned sharply to the right. It went across the street, through a large plate-glass window and ended up inside the lobby of the Parmelia Hilton International Hotel, one of the swankiest hotels in Perth. As the car settled to a stop inside the lobby, it struck a piece of furniture and righted itself, landing on all four wheels. Miraculously, no one was seriously hurt.

The doorman calmly approached the taxi and opened the back door where Samuel E. Johnson, III was sitting.

"Welcome to the Parmelia Hilton, sir," he said with a very British accent. "You had a perfectly smashing entrance."

John Dryden had a cut above his left eye and his right shirt-sleeve was ripped from the shoulder to the elbow, but rage, not pain, was in his voice as he shouted, "What the hell do you think your doin', Drake? You nearly killed all of us."

"Damn it, John, that driver was goin' to kill all of us. He was on the wrong side of the road."

"You dumb ass, Drake! He wasn't on the wrong side of the road. This ain't Oxford, this is Australia. They drive on the left side here, you damned idiot! I've a mind to bust your lip!"

"You could of at least picked the right hotel, Drake. We are staying at the Merlin," Sam added.

Sam spent the rest of the evening trying to straighten out the mess. After a trip to the police station and filling out countless insurance forms, John, Hoyt and Drake finally arrived at the Merlin Hotel. After a lengthy explanation to the rest of the crew over a few beers at the bar, everyone hit the rack. They were totally exhausted.

At eight the next morning, Perth time, the boys gathered for breakfast. They had somewhat recovered from the hellacious journey and Drake's hellacious accident.

After a filling meal, Sam Johnson decided he had better stop by the Royal Perth Yacht Club to let them know that they had arrived. There on the third floor, enclosed in a bullet proof case, sat the America's Cup; the "auld mug" as the Aussies called it. As it turned out, it was not necessary to check in. The police department had done it for him. Along with their announcement that the *Muskrat* crew had arrived, there was a strong warning from the chief that there had better not be any further trouble from the *Muskrat* crew. If there was, they would be immediately kicked out of the city. The police on the state level had also been contacted. They meant business. Sam was more than a little concerned. Besides being embarrassed by the incident, he knew fullwell that to keep Drake and the rest of the crew out of trouble would not be easy. He thought to himself, "Christ! If last evening's episode happened when they were perfectly sober, just think what could happen after a few hours in the local pub."

When Sam left for the club, the boys did a bit of exploring around Perth. Their hotel was located on the bank of the Swan River. The river was named after the lovely black swan that was indigenous to Western Australia.

Twelve miles down river at its mouth was the town of Fremantle, called Freo by the natives. It was there that the boats would be berthed. Fremantle was more or less the port of Perth. It was located on the shores of the Swan River and the Indian Ocean.

Perth had experienced a large building boom over the last couple of years, which included several new hotels. The most ambitious project was the Burswood Island Resort. This was a fancy hotel complete with a large gambling casino. The

Aussies loved to gamble. Scattered throughout Perth and Fremantle were many underground casinos, but the one at Burswood had the government's blessing.

In the Northbridge section of the city, one could find plenty of nightlife. Drake and the boys wandered around enjoying stretching their legs and not sitting in an airplane. It was a pretty morning, about seventy-five degrees and sunny. Perth was more of a city than they had envisioned. They, however, found something that nearly every town or city has. They stopped into one of the hundreds of local pubs for a few beers at about noon.

"Tinnies, gents?" the bartender asked. The boys appeared confused. The bartender explained, "A tinnie is what we call a can of beer here in Oz."

John thought that was kind of funny. "I guess that feller in the uniform we seen down there at the station last night was the wizard."

Hoyt wanted a brew, enough of the talk. "What kind you got?"

"We carry all kinds, sir."

"Give us thirteen Bud longnecks."

"I'm sorry. I don't believe we have that particular brand."

"Shee-it! What's the best beer you got?"

"I would recommend either the Swan or Fosters."

Hoyt wasn't taking to the bartender. "What do you drink bartender?"

"Personally, I drink the Fosters."

"Then we'll have thirteen Swans."

The bartender served thirteen cans of Swan Beer with a disgusted expression on his face.

After three or four rounds, the boys felt better.

"What brings you folks to Perth?" the bartender asked

Bailey Shultz.

"We're here for them cup races."

"Where are you from?"

"Oxford," Drake answered.

"Where's that?"

"It's about ten miles from Easton."

Bailey punched him in the ribs. It's amazing how Drake's ribs stood up over the years.

Bailey explained, "We're from the United States. We're sailing on one of the twelve meters."

"That's exciting. What's the name of your yacht?"

"The *Muskrat*," Drake responded. The bartender looked Bailey in the eye, waiting for a correction which was not forthcoming.

Bailey pointed to a dartboard hanging on the wall.

"You play a lot of darts in these parts?"

"Yes sir. It's almost as popular in the pubs as arm wrestling."

Drake and Bradley looked at each other and smiled. Those two men had been arm wrestling a set of oyster tongs all their lives. Both of them were very strong, and arm wrestling uses the same muscles used when tonging.

Bailey and Hambden could hold their own in darts, too. They had won the doubles championship at Dryden's several times, taking on most of the Eastern Shore.

"When do they arm wrestle in here?" Bradley inquired.

"There's not a particular time. It's usually later in the evening after everyone has quaffed a few tinnies." The boys and Allison finished their beers and at about five o'clock said goodbye.

"We may be back later tonight." Bradley said.

"G'day."

"I'll never git used to this gawd damn lingo down here, John."

"I know one thing, you'd better be used to them driving on the left side of the road or we'll all go home in little boxes or stay here and rot in jail."

Mark Litty, the first to stumble back into the hotel, spotted Sam Johnson having a drink in the bar, and sat down next to him. "Well, there's a good idea Sam. Let's have a little toddy before dinner."

Sam could tell Mark had already quaffed several. In a few seconds, the rest of the crew followed.

"Where have you boys and girls been?"

"Oh just wanderin' around Perth," Herbert said.

"Now listen to me." Sam got real serious. "I stopped by the Royal Perth Yacht Club today and the police had called them about us. They aren't going to put up with anymore trouble. They were real upset. You boys have got to behave or we'll be in a world of trouble. They called the State Police, too. I didn't spend all this money to come down here and get sent home. Now I know you've been drinking all day. Glenn, you can hardly stand up. You're gonna get in a world of trouble trying to keep up with these boys, Glenn. All of you watch yourselves. Allison, can't you keep these boys straight?"

"I'll try, Sam. But that's an impossible job sometimes."

"I had planned to take you all to The Garden at the Parmelia Hotel tonight. It's supposed to serve the best food in Perth. They say you haven't lived 'til you've tried their Lobster Chevis Regal. However, we've already been there and I think one visit is enough, at least for awhile.

"I hear 'Riccardos' is good. I didn't get any lunch so let's meet back here in an hour and we'll go." Sam went to his room to shower and change.

"I'll be here in an hour for sure," Schuyler said to the rest. "I ain't leavin'."

They all decided to stay except Allison, who went to her room and changed.

At a few minutes after seven, the group piled into three taxis and traveled to Aberdeen Street and Ricardo's. Everyone ordered a drink, and when the round came, placed their dinner orders. Sam was rather hungry. Bradley and Drake were hopeful to get back to the pub for some arm wrestling.

The food at Ricardo's was very good and the group arrived back at the Hotel by ten thirty.

Sam had planned to take everyone to Fremantle the next day, and since they were still very tired from their trip, they decided to pack it in early; everyone except Drake and Bradley, that is.

The two men wandered down to the pub to see what was going on. As they entered the front door, they saw that the place was packed. They bellied up to the crowded bar and ordered two tinnies.

They got their beer and looked around the bar. The place was filled with smoke, and the noise level from conversation was so high that you couldn't hear yourself think. In the far corner there were people throwing darts. At the end of the bar stood a table about four feet high, padded on top for arm wrestling.

"Look at that Drake! Let's git closer." As they worked their way toward the table, Bradley noticed a strange machine not far from the spot where the arm wrestling table stood.

"What's that machine, Drake?"

"Beats the shit out'a me, Bradley."

Just then a large, muscular man walked up to the machine and inserted a coin. A number of lights flashed as he gripped a long handle protruding from the top of the machine with his right hand. He placed his left hand on the machine's side and then, with all of his might tried to move the handle from his right to left.

"It's an arm wrestlin' machine, Drake!"

As he moved the handle, the number flashing on the large screen increased. At the peak of his effort, the machine read three-hundred and twenty-five.

Drake and Bradley watched as two other men approached the wrestling table. Each grabbed the other's hand and seemed to jockey their grips to see who could get the best one. A referee was there to make sure the grips were fair, and at one point, he blew a whistle to start the match. Drake and Bradley watched several matches as they drank their tinnies.

One of the men never lost. He must have defeated five or six men who had beaten three or four others for the right to wrestle him. Drake sidled up to the bartender. "Who's that feller that's winnin' all the matches there?"

"That's Blackdog. Stay clear of him. When Blackdog decides to do the lolly, (get angry), he's liable to hurt somebody badly, not to mention tear up my bar.

"A few weeks ago, Blackdog got whipped at the table. That doesn't happen too often. Blackdog was off one of the twelves. Anyway, Blackdog went after him. The boy's still in the hospital. You better stay away from 'im, myte!" Drake grabbed two beers and made his way back through the crowd toward Bradley. As he got through and made it to the wrestling table, there was Bradley looking Blackdog square in the eye. They were getting ready to go at it.

Drake hurried over to the table and leaned over in Bradley's ear. "Don't you go wrestlin' him, Bradley! His name is Blackdog and he's meaner than hell!"

"What's goin' on myte? Let's go!" Blackdog was getting angry.

"Hang on to your britches, bunky. This here's my friend." Bradley had way too much to drink and was getting a little mouthy.

"Don't you worry, Drake. This'll be like arm wrestlin' my little sister."

The people in the pub had noticed what was taking place. Upon hearing Bradley's comment, one could have heard a pin drop. Everyone took two or three steps back away from the wrestling table. It was like a crowd in a Texas bar as two gun slingers were about to have a showdown. The referee checked the grip, stepped back and blew his whistle. Blackdog put every ounce of strength he had against Bradley's right arm. Drake's eyes almost fell out onto the floor. He was drinking both beers as fast as he could.

Bradley's eyes were looking down at the table when the contest started. Blackdog's head was shaking slightly from the strain. He was red as a beet and the veins around his forehead were bulging. His eyes were bugged out as he gritted his teeth. His arm began to shake, but its position was still where it was when they started. Bradley slowly raised his head and looked Blackdog square in the eye. "Are you ready to start, bunky?"

With that, Bradley slammed Blackdog's arm to the table as if he was folding a ladder.

"Bam!" Blackdog's hand hit the table. Bradley had been playing with him. Blackdog was no match. "Now the real fight's gonna start," Drake thought to himself. He was right. Blackdog was as angry as a man could get. He yelled at Bradley, "You God damned ocker! (redneck), You're going to cark it, myte!"

"What's 'cark it' mean?" Drake asked the man next to him.

"Die!"

"Oh shee-it!"

"What's your gawd damn problem, bunky?" Bradley wasn't about to back off.

"Now mytes, let's not get into a brawl here. I'll have to call the police." The bartender was nervous, and the fact of the matter was, he had already called the cops.

"Settle down, Blackdog! He won fair and square," one of the men at the bar yelled.

"Cark him, Blackdog! " was heard from among the crowd.

The situation was getting very tense. Blackdog went for Bradley. As he made his move, another Aussie followed suit, jumping Bradley from behind. He grabbed his arms and held them behind his back as Blackdog's huge right fist glanced off Bradley's chin. Instantly, the entire pub got into the act. It was nearly even, half on Bradley's side and half on Blackdog's.

Bradley broke the man's hold who had him from behind just as Drake got to him. On his way over to Bradley's rescue, Drake ripped his beer can in two and threw half of it on the floor. He grabbed the Aussie by the hair and held his face up. Drake took the remaining half of the can and jammed it in his face, twisting it as the rough and jagged edges ripped his flesh. Blood flew everywhere.

Then it was Bradley's turn. He went berserk. Blackdog was a real bad actor. But Bradley Brown, standing at six-five, and two hundred and seventy-five pounds, was a pushover for nobody. He never looked for trouble, but when it came, he could handle himself. Bradley threw a left and missed. "Blackdog, you son-of-a-bitch!" he said.

Blackdog took another swing. It caught Bradley squarely in the right eye, and brought him to his knees. The blow sounded like a big two inch thick steak being dropped on a butcher's block. Bradley was stunned for a second, but then got up in a rage. He grabbed Blackdog by the neck with his enormous hand. He actually wrapped his hand halfway around Blackdog's size eighteen neck and with all the power he could muster, tagged Blackdog with a right. The blow was right on target and hit Blackdog's jaw with a crack. Blackdog lay on the pub floor, out cold.

Only a few seconds went by before the Perth policemen stormed the pub. There must have been thirty people in the brawl: twenty-eight Aussies fighting each other, and two boys from the *Muskrat* who had started it all.

Actually, Drake and Bradley weren't at fault. Bradley had drank a little too much, but he had challenged Blackdog at his own game and won. Blackdog had been the villain this night. That's certainly why at least half the Aussies backed Bradley in the brawl.

Nevertheless, no matter who was right or who was wrong, everyone was being put into a paddy wagon and taken to Perth City Jail. Everyone who took part in the brawl was carted off; everyone except Blackdog. During the arrests, it was determined that he had suffered a broken jaw, and he was taken off to the Perth Hospital.

At six o'clock the next morning, the chief of police called Samuel E. Johnson, III. "Mr. Johnson, you'd better come down to the station. I have two of your boys down here."

Sam couldn't believe it. "You what? That's impossible. You must be mistaken. I took my crew out for dinner last night at Ricardo's, and after that we all came back to the Merlin. I saw all of them."

"Mr. Johnson, do you know a Drake Cochran or a Bradley Brown? You must know Mr. Cochran, sir. He was on the front page of the Western Australia, our local newspaper, this morning. It was a rather unusual shot of him in the Hilton Hotel lobby. At any rate, they both are here, Mr. Johnson."

"Yes sir. I'm afraid I know them. I'll be right down." Sam thought to himself, "The boat isn't even here, and my crew will be kicked out before it arrives."

"Boys, I sure am sorry I got you all in this mess." Bradley was feeling somewhat guilty about the twenty odd Aussies sitting in the slammer with him.

"It's okay, myte. 'Tweren't your fault. You were doing no wrong."

"Ah you wowser," another Aussie on Blackdog's side piped up. "You'll pay, Mr. Brown. You'll pay by God!"

The review from the Aussies was mixed. Some wanted to be Bradley's and Drake's friend and others wanted some or all of their hides.

At six-thirty, Samuel E. Johnson, III arrived at the police station.

"Mr. Johnson, I am going to make this most brief. The night before last, I gave you fair warning that you and your *Muskrat* crew were not in great favor in the city of Perth. I must now inform you that you have twenty-four hours to rid our great city of Mr. Cochran and Mr. Brown. In fact, if this is not carried out within that time, I dare say they will be right here when you next return in a few years to try again to get back your cup.

"You and the rest of the crew may stay as long as you behave. I must say that upon reviewing your track record of the last day and a half, I would venture to guess that won't be too long.

"Now mind you, Mr. Johnson, twenty-four hours!" Sam agreed and Drake and Bradley were released.

"I'm not going to comment on this further embarrassment tonight gentlemen." Sam was utterly disgusted with the two men as they were driven back to the Merlin.

At eight-thirty, the crew gathered for breakfast before their first visit to Fremantle. They were just finishing their morning meal as Samuel E. Johnson, III appeared, looking as if he hadn't had a real good night's sleep. Sam ordered a little juice and a sticky bun.

Shortly, Drake and Bradley came from around the corner, both looking very hung over, and Bradley sporting a classic shiner around his right eye. The eye had completely closed. He was not a pretty sight. The crew knew Drake and Bradley had experienced a bad night. They only were missing the details.

When the two men sat down, Sam Johnson spoke. "Now you listen. I've spent over two million dollars to get this crew and the two boats to Australia. Do you know how long it took me to make that two million dollars? Drake and Bradley here have managed to be thrown out of Perth in less than two days. I don't think it will take the rest of you much longer if you really try.

"The boats and crew that we are against have unlimited funds and have been here for at least a year. Let's at least get our God damn boat in the water before we're eliminated. Now don't you think that's fair?"

The crew felt bad. "I'm sorry about last night, Sam." Bradley felt guilty, "We didn't do anything wrong though, Sam. I just beat a guy named Blackdog at arm wrestling and he started a fight. I promise, Sam."

"Forget who is right or wrong, Bradley. If the Perth cops can pin something on us now, we'll never get in a single race. They are on our cases boys. Believe me."

At nine thirty, they walked down to the Barrack Street Jetty and boarded the tour boat. The boat would take them on a tour down the Swan River to Fremantle, and to a small island thirteen miles off the coast.

Sam and the crew got aboard the boat for Fremantle, located twelve miles down river. As they made their way down the Swan River they were amazed at the number of boats . They learned that there were 80,000 registered boats on the Swan River alone. In Fremantle, one out of four people owned a boat. Great numbers of palatial mansions lined the banks of the Swan. It was lovely. Every once in awhile they would spot one of the black swans for which the river was named.

It would be in Fremantle, or "Freo" as the Aussies called it, that the pre-race and post-race activities would take place. There would be many a tinnie consumed at the local pubs over the next few months, and many a sea story told.

As they approached Fremantle and the mouth of the Swan River, the crew noticed the masts of the many twelves. They were berthed inside an intricate maze of breakwaters on the ocean side of town. As the boat got closer, they also got their first look at the Indian Ocean, where the battle would take place. The wind was blowing about thirty-five knots and the seas were huge as the tour boat stuck her nose out into the ocean. Old man Nick was right. It was rough as hell.

On the port side, they got a good look at the three harbors formed by the breakwaters. The closest was the The America's Cup Harbor, which was brand new. There they could see the *New Zealand* resting in her berth. Next to her the *Challenge France* and *True North'* from Canada. Very close to the jetty on their port stood a building whose sign read, Royal Perth Yacht Club Annex.

Beyond the America's Cup Harbor was The Fishing Boat Harbor, where the *Muskrat* would live for the next several months. Along with her, a number of twelves would also berth there including *South Australia, Canada II, Italia, Azzura,* plus

Kookaburra and four American syndicates; *Heart of America, Courageous, America II* and *Stars and Stripes*. It was an impressive sight to say the least.

Beyond the Fishing Boat Harbor to the south was Success Harbor. The crew could not make out the boats, but they were the *Eagle*, the *USA* and the *French Kiss*.

The sight was exciting, but it was also very intimidating to them all. There before them stood the enemy. An enemy that had been there for well over a year, with few exceptions. Those who had not been in Australia had been practicing somewhere else. Dennis Conner with his *Stars and Stripes* had been in Hawaii for months. To imagine that the United States alone had mustered seven syndicates building fifteen new boats and spending seventy million dollars to get the cup back, was mind-boggling. In all, there had been thirty-one twelve meters built since the *Australia II* took the Cup down under.

Hoyt Crane thought to himself, "I wonder if I'm in the wrong league down here. I'm scared. I've got to be careful the rest don't know it."

Thirteen miles off the coast was Rottnest Island, called "Rotto" by the locals. The name was a misnomer coming from the words "Rat's Nest." The early Dutch explorers mistook little animals called quokkas for rats. Actually, quokkas were wonderful little animals developed thousands of years ago from a combination of rats and kangaroos. The island was only seven miles long and three miles wide. No cars were allowed on the island. Transportation was mostly by bikes.

The Rottnest Hotel was the only one and is called "The Quokka Arms" by the Aussies. It was Victorian architecture and had a quaint little bar in which to 'wet your whistle'.

The tour boat made a slow circle and re-entered the Swan River. Soon the *Muskrat* crew had disembarked and found their way down to Fishing Boat Harbor. Sam located the two large slips he had leased for five months. They were right next to the *Stars and Stripes* syndicate's facility. Also included in the lease was a travel lift and a shed large enough to house *Muskrat* if necessary. The property was completely fenced in with a ten foot barbed-wire fence. He was very pleased with the facility and most anxious to have the *Oxford Queen* and *Muskrat* there. They were to arrive the next day.

"This will be home for us, gang. The *Oxford Queen* will be in this slip and the *Muskrat* here. When the ladies arrive, they will be staying right there at the P&O Hotel." He pointed up the street to the white victorian hotel on the corner with the name "P&O Hotel" painted over the entry in gold letters. On either side of the name, a glass of beer was painted and a sign that read "Swan on Tap Here." The letters for the beer ad were larger than those for the hotel.

"Now that's my kind of hotel," Drake said with a smile.

"You stay out of there, Drake. The boats will be launched tomorrow. We've got lots of work to do."

Upon inspecting their facility, the crew wandered around the docks. What they saw was fascinating. The *Stars and Stripes* was on a lift above her slip. Her keel was completely hidden by a tent arrangement. It seemed as though all the boats were very careful not to reveal their underbodies. As they wandered around, it became more and more apparent that this was not the Cedar Point Race or the Hammond Regatta. If there was a big league in the world of yacht racing, this was it.

Nearly every boat had a huge truck trailer nearby. Next to the *Stars and Stripes* were two forty-foot metal trailers painted the same blue as the boat, with the name *Stars and Stripes* in big letters painted on each side. Inside each trailer were tons and tons of gear including extra coffee grinders, sheets, blocks, halyards, winches, rudder posts, halyards, vangs, etc. Name it and it was there.

There were so many sails they were hard to count. There were nine mainsails alone. The total number of spinnakers, staysails and genoas was almost impossible to determine.

There was a sail repair area with sewing machines and tons of cloth. A long workbench with tools galore had been installed in another area.

These trailers were, of course, in addition to the large shed which was also available to the *Stars and Stripes* crew.

Next to Conner's twelve was its tender. She was a forty-foot Bertram called *Star Chaser*. She was gorgeous, with tall outriggers on either side displaying US 45 flags.

The harbor was alive with activity.

They wandered down past *Australia III's* berth. She was one of the few in the water. Two men were working on winches on deck and there was one man up the spar.

They passed the *America II*.

"Look, there's Kolius and Conner!"

John Dryden spotted them talking to each other next to the boat.

"Who?" Drake asked.

"John Kolius and Dennis Conner. There on the dock. See em, Drake?"

"Who are they, John?"

Hambden Martin spoke up. "You mean to tell me you don't know who John Kolius and Dennis Conner are, Drake? You dumb ass. Kolius is skipperin' *America II*, and Conner is at the wheel of *Stars and Stripes*. They are two of the best twelve meter skippers in the world. Conner skippered *Liberty* against the Aussies last time."

Drake shook his head, "I guess I'm confused. Did the

Aussies win last time Hambden?"

"Gawd damn it, Drake, of course they won. That's why we're here."

"Well, he may be the best in the world, but I'm glad I ain't sailin' with him. I'm glad I'm with Hoyt."

"Well thanks, Drake. That makes me feel right proud," Hoyt said.

"Well shee-it, Hoyt. That ain't nothin' to be proud about, at least you ain't never lost the Cup like he did. Why do people want to sail with him?"

"Oh shut up, Drake! Cause he's damn good, that's why. You'll find out." John was afraid Conner could hear. "We'll be racin' against him in three weeks."

The crew spent the entire afternoon looking at the twelves. Sometimes a smaller group would break off for awhile and meet up with the rest later. What they saw was very interesting, but it was also very intimidating.

Sam Johnson said to himself, "I wish old man Nick Benson could see this. I wonder if he would be intimidated like I am? I wonder if I've thrown two and a half million bucks out the window?"

The wind was really piping out of the southwest. Everyday the wind came in, usually blowing fifteen to twenty-five knots. They called it "The Fremantle Doctor." It was welcomed by the people of Freo. Without the winds, the city would be very hot and have a serious bug problem.

At about four o'clock, the crew of *Muskrat* stood by *The Eagle* in Success Harbour. They had seen every twelve except two. The *USA* and the *Azzura* were sailing off Rottnest Island where the Cup would be decided.

"Where's Drake and Bradley?" John Dryden had noticed they weren't around.

"I haven't seen them for some time, John."

"You're right, Hoyt. If those damned guys git into anymore trouble, I'll kill both of 'em."

Sam shook his head." The P&O--that's where I bet they are. Come on, let's get going. No telling what that pair is into. I need a babysitter! On second thought, I don't think they come in that size. What I need is my own jail. That pair isn't happy 'till they're in one."

The crew and Sam hurriedly made their way back to the P&O Hotel, checking in the bars on the way for the dynamic duo.

As they opened the hotel door and looked through the archway leading into the bar, they saw Drake and Bradley. Sure enough, the lure of the suds had overcome the pair again.

"You boys better be behaving yourselves!" Sam said with authority.

"Sure, Sam, you know us. Me and Bradley just stopped in for a short one!"

"Yes I do know you two. I'd sure like for you to do something a little unusual. I'd like for you to stay out of jail for awhile. That would be a little different, wouldn't it?" Drake and Bradley seemed to be okay. Besides, Sam had a little plan for them. He had made some special arrangements for later in the evening.

"Everybody sit down. I could use a cold beer myself. Bring us a round, please!" Sam treated the crew. There were six other people sitting around a table fairly close to where Drake and Bradley had been sitting. They were the only people at the bar.

"What's that funny lookin' table over there with the paddin' to it? Gawd damn thing must be five feet tall?" Vaughn had spotted the arm wrestling table.

"Maybe Bradley can help you with that one, Vaughn. Was

your performance over a table last night, Bradley?"

"Yes sir, it's for arm wrestlin', Vaughn, and that funny lookin' pinball machine over in the corner is an arm wrestlin' machine."

"Let's try it, gang. Bartender, give me some change." Vaughn headed over to the machine and dropped a coin in. He grabbed the handle and gave it everything he had. One hundred and ninety-five was the score. Next, Mark gave it a try and hit two hundred and fifty.

"Go on over there, Drake, and give it a yank." Bradley wanted to see what he could do. Drake was a powerful man. "I bet I can beat your butt." The challenge was on.

Drake dropped his coin in the machine and shrugged his shoulders. With his big right hand, he gripped the bar and held on to the side with his left. Everyone had gathered around to see the action including the six Aussies at the next table.

Drake went at it. He pulled with all his might. All of a sudden, lights started flashing and sirens started ringing. Drake pushed himself away from the machine, turned around, and bulled his way toward the archway leading out of the bar. He knocked Schuyler down as he took off. Bradley was a few feet behind Schuyler and was able to grab Drake on his way by. He put both arms around him.

"Slow down, Drake! Slow down! It ain't the cops, it's the machine! You broke the record on the machine! It's alright!"

"Gawd damn, Bradley. I thought they had me again. Right in front of Sam and everything. Scared the shit out of me!" The rest of the crew were lying in the floor laughing as were the bartender and the six Aussies.

"That calls for another round, bartender!" Hambden was buying.

Drake had scored five hundred twenty on the machine.

"Hey Bradley, you're up, honey!" The watermen of the Eastern Shore often called each other "Honey," even though it seemed a little strange for these huge men weighing two-fifty or more to be calling each by such a name.

"Let me finish my tinnie." The boys were getting into the habit of calling their beers tinnies.

Two more men came in and sat on stools at the bar. They each ordered a beer and chatted with the bartender. Both men were well over two hundred pounds, and one of them must have weighed two-eighty. He was bald and had a Fu Man Chu mustache. When he wasn't talking to the bartender, he stared at Drake with a real unfriendly expression on his face. Bradley finished his brew and stood up.

"Alright, Drake. Git a good look at that record 'cause I'm gonna break it!" Everyone again moved toward the machine.

"Wait a minute!" The bald headed man sitting at the bar stood up. "I hear we've got some men in here that think they're experts at arm wrestlin'."

Sam Johnson broke in, "Now see here gentlemen, we have to be moving along. It's getting a little late."

"Yeah. We ain't too shabby," Bradley spoke up very confidently.

The enormous hulk of a man moved toward Bradley. "I'll bet you one thousand American dollars I can top that score or the one you put on there you ocker."

Luckily, neither Drake nor Bradley knew that "ocker" meant redneck.

"You're on, bunky!" Bradley didn't back down from anybody.

"Bradley, don't get into any trouble now. Do you hear me?" Sam was as nervous as a cat.

"He's alright, Sam. Let him go. It's just a machine." John

Dryden tried to calm him down.

"Suit you, Drake? It's five hundred apiece?"

Drake looked at Bradley and thought to himself, "It's five hundred dollars worth of beer money. I'd be better off if I lost."

"Okay, Bradley, I'm in. Let's see the color of your money, bunky!"

"I'm not bunky. My name is Tanker. You call me Tanker."

Drake went to the bar and put five-one hundred dollar bills in front of the bartender. Bradley did the same. "That's a lot of arsters," they thought to themselves.

Tanker opened his wallet and pulled out a crisp thousand dollar bill and laid it on the bar. It was as if he made his living doing this. He wore a very confident smile. Bradley went to the machine and dropped in his coin. Everyone was anxiously waiting to see if he could top Drake, and wondered what would follow. Drake was happy Bradley was wrestling the machine and not Tanker. Bradley Brown gripped the bar and his left hand held the side of the machine.

"Five hundred twenty, eh? Here goes!" Bradley's muscles were enormous, and his power was devastating. With a loud grunt, he shut his eyes and pulled. If all those years of tonging oysters would ever pay off, it would be right now.

His left arm pressed against the side of the machine so hard the metal bent slightly.

The score hit six hundred and was climbing. All of a sudden, Bradley's right hand seemed to slip off the handle. He spun to his left and landed on the floor.

"Step aside!" Tanker shouted, as he headed for the machine. "Let me give you a one thousand dollar lesson, myte."

Bradley gathered himself together and got up from the floor. His nose was not six inches from Tanker's.

"Ain't nobody winnin' no money tonight, bunky."

With that, Bradley pulled from behind his back the handle he had broken off the machine.

"But count your blessin's, bunky . That could a been your arm!" Tanker couldn't believe what had happened. Had the handle weakened from overuse, or was this man really that strong?

Bradley threw the steel handle to the floor and headed for the bar to get his five hundred dollars.

"My name's not bunky! Before it's all over, you'll remember that, myte!"

Tanker vowed they would meet again.

"Let's go, boys." Sam Johnson felt he had dodged a bullet. "Let's get something to eat and get to bed early. Tomorrow the *Muskrat* arrives." The crew filed out the door, leaving Tanker and the rest in the bar. Bradley was the last to leave.

"See ya later, bunky!"

Tanker was so mad, he couldn't speak. "I'll get you, you son-of-a-bitch," he thought to himself.

As it turned out, Tanker was not an Aussie at all. He was one of the grinders on *New Zealand*, from Auckland. Bradley would meet Tanker again at sea.

Sam treated everyone to dinner at the Esplinard Hotel, the fanciest spot in Fremantle. After the meal, Sam Johnson had a couple of announcements to make.

"Gentlemen and Allison, tomorrow is a big day. The *Muskrat* will be unloaded at ten, the *Oxford Queen* right behind.

"I don't want any of you to be intimidated by the other syndicates. We may not be as fancy , but that doesn't mean they're any better. Remember one thing; none of them have beaten the *Muskrat*. I believe we have a very fast boat. In the next few weeks, we'll see just how fast. We will meet at our headquarters at Fishing Boat Harbor at nine tomorrow morning."

"Drake and Bradley, since you are no longer welcome in Perth and seem to have a wee bit of trouble staying out of jail anywhere, I will personally see you to the last ferry to Rottnest Island where I have made reservations for you tonight. Tomorrow night you will be aboard the *Oxford Queen*, of course.

"Have the desk wake you in time for the first ferry back here in the morning. John Dryden, I want you to go with that pair to Rottnest and see that they stay out of trouble. Alright? Let's get going."

Drake, Bradley and John were ferried to "Rotto" and the remaining crew went back to the Merlin Hotel in Perth with Sam.

Chapter Six

At nine the next morning, they gathered at the dock in Fishing Boat Harbor, the new home of *Muskrat*.

"How was Rottnest, boys?" Hoyt asked Drake.

"It was real good, Hoyt. I wish we was stayin' there all the time."

"Why's that, Drake? What's wrong with stayin' here?"

"Hoyt, I've been doin' a lot of lookin' and listenin', and I'm gonna let you in on a little somethin'. There's somethin' strange goin' on around here. There's somethin' real bad that ain't nobody tellin' us about."

"What the hell are you talkin' about, Drake?"

"It's the bug, Hoyt. It's the bad bug."

"What bug?"

"There's a bad bug around Fremantle, Hoyt. Matter of fact, there's more than one."

"What kind of bug are you talkin' about?"

"I ain't got the whole story yet, Hoyt, but there's these bugs going around. If you catch one of 'em, you git real sick. I hear your temperature gits real high and you could die! It's a secret though. That's why nobody's told us about it. You seen them swan in the river ain't ya? I bet they got the bug and that's what turned 'em black, Hoyt. Them swans is sick. They got the bug and there ain't neither doctor around to help."

"Drake, if there's a bug goin' around that could kill ya, why

115

wouldn't they tell ya?"

"Cause there ain't no doctors, Hoyt. That's the key to the whole problem. Ain't neither doctor will come to cure the bug."

"Gawd damn it, Drake, you're all mixed up again. What you're talkin' 'bout ain't no bug that makes you sick, it's a bug like a skeeter or ant. The doctor you been hearin' 'bout ain't the one that puts them earphones on and listens to your heart, it's the wind."

"What do you mean, the wind? How can a doctor mean the wind?"

"Drake, most everyday there's a breeze that comes up out of the southwest. They call it the Doctor, and it cools things off and blows the bugs away. That's what you've been hearin' 'bout.

"Some people call it the Fremantle Doctor. Lately it ain't come up as much and that's why it's been so hot and buggy. That's why the people's been wishin' the doctor would come. They want it to come to cool things off and git rid of the bugs, you dumb ass."

"Oh," Drake seemed relieved, "I thought we was all gonna git sick, Hoyt. The Doctor is the wind. Shee-it far."

The crew, Sam and John met at the shipping dock where the *Muskrat* and the *Oxford Queen* had been lowered into the water. Neither boat had suffered any damage. Sam had arranged for two men from Tilghman Island to accompany the boats and make sure the secret was safe. Covey Parramore and Spry Spiker were two watermen from the Island hired by Sam. They were to stay in Australia at Fishing Boat Harbor to see that the *Muskrat* was secure. They accompanied the crew as they towed the Muskrat back to the harbor. Sam, John Dryden and Hambden Martin, along with Covey and Spry, were on the

Oxford Queen. The rest made the trip aboard the *Muskrat.* They caused quite a stir as they came down the Swan River and headed out into the Indian Ocean.

Two of the crew of *Australia III* were sitting in the Royal Perth Yacht Club Annex. "There's the other twelve, myte! Unusual name I'd say. What does bloody *Muskrat* mean?"

It was fairly rough in the ocean as they headed into the seas. "Look at her, myte! She doesn't seem to hobby horse, does she?"

As the *Muskrat* was being put in her slip, a crowd gathered beyond the fence and the neighboring docks. There were quite a few comments about the placement of the cockpit and the forward lockers. People also wondered where the coffee grinders were and most of all, what was a *Muskrat.*

The crew went right to work putting the spar in the boat. Sam had arranged for a crane for stepping the mast. It went in without any problems. As the strut was put in place over the transom, and the backstay was in place, there was quite a stir from the crowd. No one could figure what the unusual arrangement was all about.

The biggest stir, however, came when the boom was installed. How could it be legal for Muskrat to have a boom eight feet longer than any other twelve.

The crew worked all day on the boat. Those not on the twelve unloaded the gear from the *Oxford Queen* into the shed. Some of the sails were placed aboard the twelve.

At fivethirty, John Dryden yelled to everyone, "All right, gang, come on over here. I got something for you!"

As the crew headed up the dock, they found a wonderful sight: a tub of shaved ice filled with a couple of cases of Budweiser longnecks which had been stowed on the *Queen.* They thoroughly enjoyed their beer and at about seventhirty,

Sam decided it was time to get something to eat. "Put your gear on the *Queen* boys and let's get some dinner. We've got some sailing to do tomorrow."

After dinner, the crew went back to the *Oxford Queen* for the night. They had put in a good day's work. Sam Johnson went to his room at the Esplinard Hotel.

Bradley, Drake and Hoyt wandered up to the P&O bar for a beer before hitting the rack. The place was packed. It seemed the P&O was one of the favorite bars of the sailors and there were quite a few twelve meter boys there. One of topics of conversation that night was the *Muskrat.*

"Where the hell is that syndicate from?" someone asked.

"United States, I think," the guy next to him replied.

Hoyt was sitting close by the two. He thought they were Aussies. "She's from Oxford, Maryland. Where are you guys from?"

"Auckland, myte! We're on the *New Zealand.* Do you know her?"

"Yeah, nice looking boat."

"You on a twelve, myte?"

"The *Muskrat*, the one you just asked about."

"What kind of backstay is on that boat, Myte?"

"It's so we can carry that long boom. She carries a right smart main you know."

Bradley asked the *New Zealand* boys a question. "You boys know somebody named Tanker?"

"Oh you got that right, myte. He's one of our grinders. You know Tanker, do you?"

"Yeah, I know of him. Next time you see him, tell him his bunky said hi."

"You're lookin' for trouble, Bradley. I'll tell you that." Drake was not very happy.

The boys had a couple more beers. Even though there were several arm wrestling matches taking place, Hoyt convinced Drake and Bradley to stay away. At about midnight, they wandered back to the *Queen* and went to sleep.

After breakfast, the crew boarded the *Muskrat*, and Spry maneuvered the *Oxford Queen* out of her slip. She hooked up with *Muskrat* and towed her out through the breakwaters into the ocean for her maiden sail. Everyone was excited about finally putting some sail on the boat. Some of the competition jumped on their tenders and followed them out. They were anxious to see the unusual rig in action.

As the *Oxford Queen* moved well out into the ocean, she headed upwind. The crew aboard *Muskrat* raised the huge mainsail. Schuyler went forward and tossed the towline to the *Queen*. For the first time, the *Muskrat* was on her own.

The wind was around twenty knots. Hoyt called for the heavy number one and Hambden agreed. It was close to the number two genoa, which was placed in the starboard fore-deck locker. The port locker was left empty. "Fire her up!" Hoyt called for the heavy number one to be hoisted up the forestay.

The four men below went to work on the rowing winches. The heavy number one was up in less than five seconds.

One of the crew that had jumped on their tender was that of the English challenger, *Crusader*. "Did you see that sail go up? Christ! It must be done electrically. That's illegal!"

No one could believe the speed of the sail on the hoist.

"Trim the jib! Allison, let's get the main in!" Hoyt called for sail trim. Bailey put the jib trim in slow gear. It was trimmed very gradually. "Let's go slow on the trimming speed for a while, Bailey. I don't want to tear anything up." The *Muskrat* gained speed as she reached out toward the northwest. Before long she was boiling, doing a good fifteen knots.

"Gawd damn, Hambden, she's walkin' the dog!" Hoyt was excited about her speed. Back on the *Queen*, Sam and John were just as excited. She looked beautiful as she cut through the seas, her big mainsail powering her along with her high cut jib not taking on a single wave.

"Let's put her on the wind," Hoyt yelled.

Hambden called for slow trim as the boat headed closer to the wind. The *Muskrat* lost some speed, as was expected by sailing closer to the wind, but she was still very fast.

Everyone was pleased with the boat's performance. The *Muskrat* handled the weather work well. It was blowing around twenty over the deck and seemed to be building.

"The Doctor arrived today didn't she, Drake!" Hoyt yelled below.

"How the hell would I know? Have we left the harbor?"

Drake was still upset he had to stay below.

As it breezed up to close to thirty knots, Hambden suggested the number two. "Let's go to the number two and see how these lockers work."

Schuyler, Vaughn and Jimmy got out of their cockpit, and Sky opened the hatch and secured the halyard to the number two. Vaughn tied on the backup sheet.

"Go!" Schuyler yelled to the boys below.

Bailey put the halyard in high gear and in about four seconds the number two was up. Jimmy released the halyard on the heavy number one and let it down. It went neatly into the locker. Jimmy untied the halyard and closed the locker. In less than a minute, the sail change was completed and the foredeck crew were back in their weather cockpit. Sam and John Dryden were ecstatic.

"Damn, John! That was unbelievable! No muss, no fuss!

That didn't take a minute. That Nick Benson is a genius."

The boys from *Crusader* had the same reaction. "How did they do that? How did they make that bloody change?"

Back on the *Muskrat*, Hambden and Hoyt were all smiles. "I bet them boys ashore are sayin' somethin', Hambden."

"You got that right, Hoyt. Let's put the number three in the other locker, boys."

After the number three was placed in the locker, Hambden thought they might be getting a little close to the reefs off Rottnest Island.

"We'd better roll her, Hoyt. We'll be on a reef if we don't."

"Ready about!" Hoyt yelled to the crew.

"Let's see how good you boys are at rowing! Hard alee!" Hoyt turned the wheel as Pete Dillon released the jib. Allison slid the boom down the traveller as the *Muskrat* came head to wind. Hoyt had turned the wheel hard and the jib quickly cleared the mast.

"Trim!" Bailey yelled to the boys below. He had the drum on high speed. It seemed there was never any slack in the leeward sheet. It snapped aft so quickly it was as though the sail was on a huge rubber band. It was completely in by the time Hoyt could get the *Muskrat* on course.

Nobody had ever seen a boat of that size tack so quickly.

"It's scary, Bailey," Hambden yelled. "We don't have to worry about getting the sail in with Nick's invention. We got to worry about rippin' it on the spreader or pullin' the sheet out of the clew."

The boys on the *Crusader* tender were flabbergasted.

"That bloody twelve tacks like a sunfish, myte. I've never seen the likes of it! Forget a tacking duel with her. I can't bloody believe it! What kind of winches are on that boat?"

No one could believe it. The power generated by the men

below on their shell arrangements was unheard of in racing history. Nick was brilliant.

As the *Muskrat* slid along on port tack, she eventually got within view of the people on shore and caused quite a stir. She was unlike any twelve they had ever seen. Her long boom sticking out over her transom and her high cut jib were very unusual.

All of a sudden, with no warning at all the crew, heard the deafening noise of a helicopter. The chopper was directly over the boat and came within what appeared to be a few feet from the top of the spar. A cameraman was hanging out of its door, filming the *Muskrat* below.

"Go head to wind, Hoyt. Ease the jib! Head to wind, Hoyt!"

Hoyt could barely hear Hambden's orders above the noise of the chopper, but he headed into the wind. The chopper continued to hover and the cameraman continued to film.

"Jib down!" Hambden barked, "Don't let this boat heel, Hoyt! They're trying to take pictures of her bottom! Wave to the *Queen!* Get her over here! Jib down, boys!"

Hoyt kept just enough air in the main to keep her moving as the *Oxford Queen* came close by. Soon the *Muskrat* was under tow, heading back to "Freo."

"They ain't gonna learn the secret that easy," Hambden said to Hoyt.

"Good thinkin', Hambden!" Hoyt was damn glad he had figured out what was going on.

"I heard about that chopper in the P&O two nights ago. It belongs to Channel 7 news, a T.V. channel in Perth. It filmed all the twelves up close. There's a move afoot among the challengers to make it illegal for the chopper to get closer than a hundred yards of a twelve. They're tryin' to get a law passed. They've gone to the Royal Perth Yacht Club and all.

"Seems as though the owner of *Australia III* , Owen Brewer, also owns Channel 7 News."

"What can we do about our secret, Hambden? We got to sail. If we sail, we gotta heel, and if we heel and a chopper is on top of us, its all over." Hoyt was very concerned.

By now everyone had gathered around Hoyt at the helm. Schuyler Mattingly spoke up. "I know what we can do. I've got a plan."

"What's that, Sky?"

"We got to go up in a chopper and look at a twelve like they did. If we do, I can solve the problem. Just get me in a chopper." They would discuss this with Sam when they tied up. As they came into Fishing Boat Harbor, people were pouring into the area where the *Muskrat* was berthed.

When the *Muskrat* was finally tied safely in her slip, there must have been three or four hundred people gawking at the boat from behind the fence and on nearby docks.

You could hear the crowd, "Did you see her tack? She's fast myte! It was blowin' thirty with some big seas and she didn't hobby horse. I'd like to get on her! She could be the break-through!"

The press nearly tore down the gate to get in. Covey Parramore and Spry saw that they didn't.

The *Muskrat* crew was both very excited and very concerned. They loved the way the *Muskrat* performed and loved all of the attention they were getting. On the other hand, they were very concerned about divulging their secret. Even though the *Muskrat* had sailed only once very briefly, it seemed she was a very special boat. They didn't want anybody to know just how special she was.

Sam Johnson went to the main gate and spoke with the reporters. He was not prepared for such a welcoming committee. He suggested they meet him in a room which was part of the boat shed in a few minutes. He also explained that they would not be permitted to get on board the *Muskrat*, and asked if there was anyone there from Channel 7 News. When he found there was a reporter from the station, he pulled him aside.

"Was that your chopper over us today?"

"Yes sir," the reporter answered.

"You are welcome to join the rest of the reporters, but I must warn you, if your chopper ever does again what it did today, you or anyone else from Channel 7 News will be banned."

"I understand, sir. I'm very sorry."

Sam Johnson and Hoyt Crane met with the press. When everyone settled down, Sam spoke. Hoyt had never taken part in a press conference before. "My name is Samuel E. Johnson, III and this is Hoyt Crane. I am the owner of the *Muskrat* and Hoyt is the skipper.

"We, and the entire crew, are from the state of Maryland in the U.S., and live in or near a little town called Oxford. Oxford is a town of about eight hundred people and is located on the shores of the Chesapeake Bay. Now, we'll do the best we can to answer any questions."

"Did you say that the entire crew of the *Muskrat* i s basically from the same town of eight hundred people?"

"That is correct."

"Who designed the *Muskrat* ?"

Sam answered, "Mr. Nicholas Benson was her designer."

"Where is his firm located?"

"In Oxford."

Someone else asked, "Who did you have build the boat, Mr. Johnson?"

"The boat was built by Nick Benson."

"Where is his yard located?"

"Oxford." Sam replied.

There were several comments among the reporters, but neither Sam nor Hoyt could make out what was being said.

"Where were your spars made, Mr. Harrington?"

"The Oxford Boatyard, sir." This response brought a few chuckles from the press.

From the back row, a reporter with a very French accent asked, "Who did you choose to make your sails, Mr. Johnson?"

"A gentleman by the name of Downes Hackett made our sails for us."

"I guess his loft is in Oxford. Right, Mr. Johnson?"

"That's right, down on Tilghman Street." The press got a good laugh out of that.

"Why won't you permit anyone on the *Muskrat*? What's the big secret all about?"

Sam took his time answering. "Gentlemen, the *Muskrat* is the result of a very unusual design. Some of the innovations, like the placement of the cockpit and backstay arrangement are obvious. There are other innovations like her coffee grinders and underbody that aren't so obvious. We've decided to keep these to ourselves for a while."

"When will you disclose these secrets, Mr. Johnson?" asked another reporter.

"You will be welcome aboard the *Muskrat* when we are either eliminated or win the America's Cup. I hope it's the latter."

Hoyt and Sam answered the reporters' questions for another forty minutes, then concluded the press conference.

The next morning there was a picture of the *Muskrat* on the front page of the "Perth Gazette" under the caption, "Latest Challenger Looks Fast".

The article described the *Muskrat* and her first day in the Indian Ocean. It also pointed out that she was very much unproven and as of this date hadn't beaten anybody.

The films of the *Muskrat* taken by Channel 7 News did not reveal her underbody.

Schuyler Mattingly took a chopper ride the next morning and followed the *French Kiss* over the race course. Upon his return, he arrived back at the dock with four gallons of a very thin paint developed especially for the twelves. The paint he had was a little different from the rest, however. It had been tinted, and was the exact color of the Indian Ocean. It would be very difficult to distinguish the bottom of the boat from the waters of the ocean once she was painted.

The *Muskrat* went out every day for two weeks. They sailed in almost every condition the ocean could throw at them. They sailed in five knots up to forty. Most of the time the winds blew fairly hard. The Fremantle doctor seemed to make his rounds nearly daily. So far Nick was right on the money. The *Muskrat* seemed to go very well in anything above eighteen. Below eighteen, especially around ten to twelve knots, she didn't move as well. As a matter of fact she seemed sluggish in light air, but they weren't concerned.

Everyone was very excited about the *Muskrat*. She and the 'Doctor' seemed to get along very well.

October fifth was only two days away. That marked the beginning of the round robin. Over the next four months, there would be an incredible four hundred races sailed in the waters off Fremantle.

The *Muskrat* was scheduled to go against the *Eagle* on Sunday. It would be Sam battling his dear friend Commodore Ewing Brown head to head in *Muskrat's* first race. Sam would much prefer anybody else, but such was the luck of the draw.

It was Friday, October third; *Muskrat* would not go out that Saturday. The boys could relax.

With the exception of Schuyler, the crew met at the P&O Hotel for breakfast. The hotel had turned into their hangout. It was a favorite spot for most of the sailors. As they entered the dining room, the boys from the *Stars and Stripes* were buzzing. "You guys hear about what happened last night to the French boat?"

No one from the *Muskrat* group had heard a word.

"Someone got into her compound during the night and apparently got under her cover and got several pictures."

Mark Litty had seen the security at the compound. He couldn't believe anyone could penetrate it. "How in the hell did anybody get through their security system? They had several guards and two of the meanest Dobermans I've ever seen."

"The dogs were shot and at least one of the guards was badly beaten. I don't know all the details. The police are investigating."

"Jesus Christ! Somebody's playin' for keeps. There hasn't been a race and they're killin' dogs and beating up people!"

"Hell, Bradley and Drake 'been beatin' up on people since the first day they was here." Hoyt couldn't resist the comment.

"That was different, Hoyt. They started that stuff. Do the cops have any leads?" Drake asked.

"I'm not really sure, but I hear they're goin' to question every syndicate."

"That makes sense, I guess." Drake turned to Hambden sitting across the table. "I hope nobody can get to the *Muskrat*."

Sam had a worried look and was thinking of what he could do to beef-up security.

"I'll tell you one gawd damn thing," Hambden said with

great confidence, "if anybody tries to git to the *Muskrat* and runs into Spry and Covey, the police will git called all right. It'll be 'bout a murder; them boys will kill'em."

Sam wasn't as confident. "You boys keep your ears and eyes open when you're on the *Queen*. If anybody notices anything, ring the hell out of that bell."

The boys finished their breakfast and each went their separate ways. Sam and John went back to the compound to bring Spry and Covey up to date. Sam also wanted to discuss some extra precautions. Drake and Bradley took Mark, Hambden and Allison down to the Barrack Street jetty and boarded the ferry to Rottnest Island. The rest decided to wander around the harbor and see what was happening with the other twelves.

Drake and Bradley hadn't been to the island since they stayed there for the night several weeks before. It was the first visit for Mark, Hambden and Allison.

The trip to Australia had not been easy for Allison. It was sometimes difficult to be the only female in the group. She in fact, was the only female that would sail on any of the twelves. She wished the girls from home were flying down earlier. Even though she was originally from Western Pennsylvania, she had sailed all of her life. As a child, her mother and father would pack her and her two sisters into the car and tie the sunfish her father had made on top. They would drive for hours to find a suitable lake where they would sail for the day. When Allison was in college, she was the captain of the sailing team, and shortly after graduation won the 470 Nationals. Allison was not only an excellent mainsail trimmer, she would often catch the jib or spinnaker trimmer not paying attention and get them on the ball. She was thrilled to be a member of the *Muskrat* crew. This surely was to be the highlight of her long sailing career.

They arrived on the island at twelve fifteen and wandered up to the hotel for a sandwich. After lunch and two or three Swan drafts, they rented bicycles and toured the island. At five thirty, they caught the ferry back to Fremantle.

Upon their return, as they approached the gate to the compound, they saw the crew and Sam Johnson gathered around someone. Sam seemed very upset and as they got closer, could hear what he was saying. He was very angry, waving his finger in some stranger's face. "You bring that God damn chopper close to my boat one more time and there's going to be big trouble! You bastards weren't ten feet above her spar today, kicking up dust everywhere! You damn near ripped the canvas that hides her bottom! There should be a law about something like that! You do it one more time and that chopper will never fly again! You tell Mr. Brewer or whoever else you want what I said!"

The gentleman to whom he was speaking was a representative of Channel 7 News. Appparently, their helicopter had come over the harbor and hovered very close to the *Muskrat*. Sam was there at the time and called the police. They arrived, but could do nothing. Sam then called the news station. As a result, they sent this man down to the boat.

The crew was also very angry. John Dryden was among them. "I can knock a pair of canvasbacks out goin' downwind in thirty knots buster, and you can bet your sweet ass I can hit that chopper. Bring that son-of-a-bitch back here and I'll show you right now!"

The representative sent by Channel 7 News was very patient. "I'm very sorry for this most unfortunate incident, gentlemen. As I have previously stated, to my knowledge the chopper has orders to stay a safe distance from the twelves. I promise you the pilot will be reprimanded and I assure you this will not happen again."

"It better not." Sam was still angry, but sensed the newsman was in a no-win situation. "I do thank you for coming."

"Again, I'm sorry."

The newsman went to his car.

"Did they see anything, Sam?"

"I don't think so, Hambden. I wish I knew what the hell was going on though; the French last night and another attempt to unlock our secret today. I wonder if Brewer could be behind this?"

"Well gawd damn, Sam, it's his chopper ain't it?"

"Yeah, Drake, but I can't believe he would do anything like that. Owen Brewer is a class act. I don't think it's him."

"Could it be someone else in his syndicate?"

"I guess anything's possible, Drake. Someone has made up their mind to learn a few things they shouldn't. I hope they find out who it is soon. Meanwhile, I want you to take shifts helping Spry and Covey. No way two men can do the job. I want three people helping them around the clock 'till I can figure something else out."

It was seven o'clock when they walked to the P&O for dinner. Jimmy Firth, Glenn Parrot and Vaughn Downes stayed behind with Spry to guard the boat. After their meal, Sam pleaded with the crew to go straight back to the *Queen* and get a good night's sleep for the race. Sam went back to the Esplinard Hotel for the night.

The bartender spotted Drake and Bradley. He came over to their table carrying a legal size pad of paper and a pen.

"Hey, mytes! We got the wrestling machine fixed for ya!"

He would never forget Bradley's breaking off the handle.

"The big arm wrestling tournament starts next week. Why don't you two sign up? Two men on a team, hundred dollar entry fee, winner takes all. The prize is five thousand dollars."

"Shee-it, Bradley! We gotta sign up for that!"

"Yeah, Drake. But don't none a you boys tell Sam 'bout this. He'd kill us."

Bradley and Drake signed up for the tournament. Their first match was Tuesday night at eleven o'clock. After a couple more beers, they headed back to the boat. Three men relieved the crew on guard and the rest went aboard the *Queen* for some sleep.

At seven-thirty the next morning, they were aboard the *Muskrat* getting ready for their race with *Eagle*. The race was to start at noon. Fortunately, there had been no trouble during the night.

The wind was out of the southeast blowing about twenty and building. The sky was clear and the seas were high.

At nine o'clock, Sam arrived and met with the crew aboard the *Queen*. "Well, boys, this is it. Today we go against *Eagle*. A lot has happened since we saw her in Newport. This is going to be the first race for the *Muskrat*. I believe in her and I believe in each of you. Good luck!"

Not a word was spoken as Hoyt and the crew boarded the twelve.

At ten o'clock, the *Eagle* was towed out of Success Harbor and at ten-twenty, the *Oxford Queen* and the *Muskrat* left the inlet and entered the Indian Ocean.

Hambden Martin was so excited that his mouth was dry. To think that he was the tactician on a twelve meter. He would be calling the shots. If he made a mistake, it could cost his country the Cup.

Chapter Seven

The spectator fleet numbered around fifty to seventy-five boats varying in all types and sizes. The smaller boats rocked and hobby-horsed frantically in the heavy seas.

The race committee was already on station, since this was the second of three races that would be sailed on Sunday. In the first race, Dennis Conner's *Stars and Stripes* had beaten the Canadian challenger *True North* by twenty-seven seconds. The last race would be between the *New Zealand* and the *Crusader*.

The committee boat for the day was a forty-three-foot custom built motor yacht with a dark blue hull and varnished cabin. She had a small flying bridge. The race committee, dressed in white ducks and blue blazers each sporting a white captain's hat, looked very spiffy with the various race committee flags in the air overhead.

As the *Oxford Queen* and *Muskrat* passed the *Eagle*, Sam could see Commodore Ewing Brown on the bridge of his tender *Wings*. The Commodore tipped his hat to the *Queen*, "Good luck, Sam."

Sam, in turn, waved his hat in the air. "Good luck to you Commodore, I hope you come in second!" As the Queen of England learned many years ago—in the America's Cup there is no second. The commodore smiled.

At eleven thirty, the main was hoisted on *Muskrat* and her

tow line taken back aboard the tender. She was on her own.

Hampden Martin barked orders to the foredeck crew, "Heavy number one on deck! Number two in the starboard locker, number three in the port."

The *Eagle* already had her headsail up. It was her number two. The *Muskrat* was gambling they could carry more sail. "Fire her up, Sky!" The genoa streaked up the head stay. "Lots of halyard tension."

The *Queen* and *Wings* powered away from the starting area as the ten minute gun fired. Hoyt felt a few butterflies, he knew it was time to perform. No more theories, no more talk. This was the moment everyone had been waiting for, from the people at Brinkley's and Dryden's back in Oxford who felt it was their *Muskrat*, to Samuel E. Johnson, III who had put up the money. The moment of truth had finally arrived.

The *Muskrat* sailed to the committee boat and tacked. She was being followed by *Eagle*, with Rod Davis at the helm. He was one of the world's best. Davis would be tough at the start. As the five minute gun fired, the *Muskrat* jibed and headed away from the line on port tack, and *Eagle* was right on her transom. "Let's go hard on the wind," Hambden yelled to the crew.

The wind was holding at twenty knots. Hambden was happy with his sail selection. As the *Muskrat* went hard on the wind, *Eagle* hardened up with her and was to weather. With two minutes to go, they were heading back toward the line.

They got within three boat lengths of the starting line when *Muskrat* tacked over to starboard and slowly eased sheets and jibed. The *Eagle* was ten yards behind her, imitating her every move. It was like a dog chasing its tail. The *Eagle* and *Muskrat* slowly circled each other two boat lengths from the starting line. It was a game of cat and mouse.

With ten seconds to go to the gun, Davis' *Eagle* went for the start. He was between *Muskrat* and the starting line having just gone on starboard tack. *Muskrat* followed, but Davis had beat them to the punch and as the gun sounded was two boat-lengths dead to weather of the *Muskrat. Muskrats'* jib was luffing as the gun sounded. They had lost the start badly.

"Head off and get her goin', Hoyt."

"Alright, Hambden. Ease the jib and main a hair."

The *Eagle* won the start by about four or five boat lengths. That's a lot in these races, especially with the shorter legs.

As the boat got her speed up, Hambden told Hoyt to tack. "Ready about! Hard alee!" Hoyt threw the wheel over.

"Let's see what Rod can do tackin' with us."

The *Muskrat* tacked on a dime and surprisingly didn't loose her speed. As soon as the *Muskrat* tacked, the *Eagle* went with her. Unlike the *Muskrat*, she seemed to hobby-horse as she went head to wind. When both boats had completed their tacks, the *Muskrat* had gained half a boat length.

"Gawd damn if this boat can't tack, boys," Hambden yelled to the boys on the rowing winches. "We've gained half a boat length, Drake! Keep them oars a rowin', boys. Are you ready for another one?"

"Gawd damn right!" Drake could work that machine all day.

"Ready about. Hard alee." Hoyt rolled the wheel over again. The jib snapped back as if it were on huge rubber bands. The sail was trimmed in before the men below realized it. The amazing thing was the boat didn't lose speed in the middle of the tacks. Usually when a boat comes head to wind (directly into the wind), it loses speed rapidly. Because of the little time it took to trim the jib, the boat didn't slow down at all. The *Eagle* covered the *Muskrat*. Again when she went head to wind, she hobby-horsed a couple of times in the seas. During this tack, she lost over half a boat length. The *Muskrat* was on the move.

"I guess the Commodore ain't never heard of no ruddynut, eh, Hoyt?" Hambden was ecstatic.

"Guess so, Hambden. We're solid eatin' her up, ain't we?" The boys below could hear the conversation. "Git'em Hoyt!" Bradley yelled up to the cockpit.

The *Muskrat* held her tack for about two minutes.

"Ready about!" Hoyt saw Hambden's signal to go.

"Hard alee!"

The *Eagle* covered. This time she lost about a quarter of a boat length. It was obvious she couldn't tack with the *Muskrat*.

The two boats tacked again, and this time the *Muskrat* broke through. The Eagle no longer was sitting on her air. As Hoyt held his position, his boat seemed to crawl to weather ever so slowly.

Hoyt rounded the weather mark slightly ahead of the *Eagle*. The next leg was dead downwind. This is where she was really supposed to shine. Her big main would really pay off now.

The foredeck crew did an excellent job getting the ounce-and-a-half spinnaker up. It was drawing while the boat still had an overlap on the mark.

"Now watch us go, Davis!" Hoyt was absolutely thrilled. He had beaten the *Eagle* to the first mark after losing the start, and now they were doing what the boat did best — running.

The pole was set to starboard at the mark. Hoyt held low. He felt he had enough air to keep her moving. It had piped up to about twenty-two or three.

The *Eagle* rounded the mark only ten yards behind. Her crew also did a great job with the chute.

After about five minutes on the running leg, the *Eagle* jibed. Hambden was watching their every move. "Let's jibe gang.

We got to stay between her and the mark. I ain't makin' that mistake. Ready, Allison?"

"Trim the main amidships. Let's go, Sky!" Hoyt brought the boat dead downwind as Allison trimmed the main amidships and the foredeck crew jibed the chute.

"Made!" Jimmy yelled. He was the point man on the foredeck. He actually placed the new guy into the jaws of the spinnaker pole. When the after guy was in, he yelled "Made!" and Hambden brought the pole aft.

"Nice jibe, boys." Hoyt was very happy with their performance and position. They had opened up about four boat lengths on the *Eagle* since rounding the weather mark.

Sam Johnson was as excited as anybody aboard the *Oxford Queen.*

"Look at her, John! She's pulled well ahead. I sure wish Old Man Nick was here."

"Me too, Sam. That's the prettiest sight I've seen since Allison lost her bathing suit top at the beach."

Just as it seemed everything was going perfectly, Hambden Martin popped everyone's bubble. "How's our trim? The Eagle's gainin' on us."

Bailey had the spinnaker sheet. "It's out as far as she'll go. The pole is fine, Hambden."

The *Eagle* was closing the gap rapidly.

"Check for grass, Pete! There's somethin' wrong!"

"There's no grass, Hambden. I've already checked."

"Maybe our rudder is fouled."

Sam became very uneasy aboard the *Oxford Queen.* "What's wrong out there, John? The *Eagle* is closing fast!"

"Maybe she's just bringin' up her own air, Sam."

"The air looks steady to me, John."

Hambden kept looking aft. Every time he turned around

the Eagle was closer. "Bring her up a little, Hoyt. See if we can get a little speed on. Pole forward a hair. Watch your trim, Bailey. Just bring her up a couple of degrees." Hoyt came up slightly.

"Hold her there Hoyt."

The *Eagle* held her course. She was still closing the gap.

"We can't stay up like this or we'll have to jibe back out." Hambden was afraid he would end up on the wrong side of the leeward mark.

"Bring her down to the mark, Hoyt. Pole aft, Pete. Be ready to ease, Bailey."

The Eagle had not changed her course. After her jibe, she headed directly for the mark, giving her a better angle. The *Muskrat* was now dead downwind. At times, she was sailing by the lee.

As they approached the mark, the *Eagle* passed the *Muskrat*.

"What's wrong out there John? She was going so well before the jibe."

"Beats me, Sam. We'll get'em on the weather leg!"

"I hope so, but Nick built this boat to reach and run! I think something's wrong."

As the *Eagle* doused her chute and rounded the leeward mark, she was five boat lengths ahead of *Muskrat*. The wind had strengthened to twenty-five knots and the seas were building.

Hambden had called for the number two prior to rounding. The heavy number one was stowed in the starboard locker. *Muskrat* rounded the leeward mark twenty-five seconds behind the *Eagle*. Rod Davis had made up nearly a minute on the downwind leg. Something was definitely wrong.

"Alright, you boys below, get ready. We're gonna see how bad those boys want to cover us. Hambden wanted a tacking duel. Ready about! Hard alee!" Hoyt tacked the twelve. The *Muskrat* was amazingly steady, barely hobby-horsing at all. The jib was trimmed with incredible speed.

The *Eagle* covered, staying between *Muskrat* and the mark. By doing this, they accomplished two things. First they forced the *Muskrat* to sail in disturbed air, since the *Eagle* was directly to weather of her. Secondly, it prevented *Muskrat* from finding a wind shift that gave them an advantage. As long as the *Eagle* was in the same area, or the same side of the course, both boats would experience the same shifts. However, if the *Eagle* went on the opposite side of the course from *Muskrat*, it would be a big gamble. The problem Rod Davis and the *Eagle* were having is that every time both boats tacked, the *Muskrat* gained ground.

As soon as the boats settled down, Hambden was ready to go again. "Ready about! Hard alee!"

The *Muskrat* went back on port tack. In a few seconds, the *Eagle* covered. She was less than four boat lengths ahead. Hambden's plan was working.

"Alright Hoyt, let's go!"

"Ready about! Hard alee." Hoyt tacked the boat again, followed immediately by Davis.

It was quite exciting to watch. Davis's boat had a brightly colored eagle, trailing the American flag in its talons, painted on each side of the grey hull. Spray flew as they worked their way to the mark, tacking every minute or two.

Rod Davis was one of the masters at match racing. Davis had proven that at the Congressional Cup Series. He had proven it again at the start. Lowell North and Bill Ficker were advisors to the *Eagle*. She was smartly sailed.

As the two boats beat to weather in heavy seas, it became obvious that the *Muskrat* was steadily closing the gap. About three quarters up the weather leg, she was clear ahead of *Eagle* by about three boat lengths on port tack. This time the *Eagle* tacked first. Now it was the *Muskrats'* turn to cover. She tacked with Eagle.

Within two minutes, the *Eagle* went again. This time, Hambden waited until he was almost dead to weather of her. "Roll her, Hoyt." They sat on *Eagle* to the weather mark, tacking eight more times. When they rounded and set the chute, they had opened up a forty-two second lead. The *Muskrat* had shown exceptional speed.

Bill Ficker was aboard the *Eagle*. "That boat's as fast as greased lightning, Rod. Who's sailing her?"

"I've never heard of the boat. I've never heard of the owner or the skipper. But I'll tell you one thing, a lot of people are going to know about her if she keeps sailing with that kind of speed. Look how high her jib's cut. "

The *Eagle* set her chute. They were on the fourth leg of the race which was a reaching leg. The boat would round the reaching bouy on starboard tack, and then jibe over to port and go for the leeward mark. The *Muskrat* took off on this leg. She literally left Davis and the *Eagle* in her wake. It was an honest leg. Both boats were on starboard tack, reaching for the mark.

"This boat is solid walkin', Allison." Glenn Parrot was very pleased with what they were doing to the *Eagle*.

"I can tell you one thing, this main has some power today." Allison had her hands full.

Back aboard the *Oxford Queen*, Sam and John were watching every second of the race. "I don't get it Sam. Now she's killing the *Eagle* downwind. I mean she's eatin' her up. I don't understand."

The reaching legs offered very little chance for tactics in the twenty-five knot breeze. *Muskrat* had a comfortable lead, and led *Eagle* to the jibing mark. Hoyt jibed the boat around the mark nearly two minutes ahead of *Eagle*. "We're killin' 'em, gang. Damned if we ain't killin' 'em. Gawd damned Eastern Shore boys are showin' 'em somethin'." Hoyt was tickled to death.

After four minutes into the next leg, Hambden became concerned again, "Look at our speed, we've lost over a knot and the wind's picked up over the deck. Check for weed!"

Mark checked, but found nothing. "Ain't no weed, Hambden!" The boat was really slow and the *Eagle* was coming on fast.

"What the hell's going on?" Hoyt was very concerned. "She's stopped. There's got to be grass on her somewhere!" There was lots of grass in the area, but no one could detect any on *Muskrat*.

"Did you look at the rudder?" Hambden yelled below.

There was a window that allowed Mark to see the forward edge of the rudder. "Yeah, nothin!" Mark had already checked. The sails were perfectly set, and Hoyt was steering right for the mark. If the air had changed at all in strength, it had increased. Its direction had not budged. There was no grass slowing down the *Muskrat*.

"Damn it, Hambden! What the shit's wrong with this bucket? We picked up over a minute on *Eagle* on the last leg. What's wrong? The *Eagle* was picking up a boat length every thirty seconds.

"I don't git it, Sam. The gawd damn boat kills the *Eagle* on the first reachin' leg and now this. Don't make neither bit of sense."

Sam was in a state of shock. "Beats me, John. I can't believe what I'm seeing."

Hambden tried not to lose his cool. "Just hang in there now.

We'll figure this out." He kept looking around, trying to find something that would be slowing the *Muskrat* down.

The *Eagle*, by this time, was one boat length behind.

"Let's go up, Hoyt! Make her pass to leeward."

The *Eagle* passed to leeward and was sailing in clear air in less than a minute. The *Muskrat* had lost nearly two knots of speed. She rounded the leeward mark nearly five minutes behind the *Eagle*. Things did not look good.

"Drake, you boys get ready! We'll be doin' lots of tackin'! Let's go Hoyt."

"Ready about! Hard alee!"

The *Muskrat* tacked about every minute. On every tack, she gained on the Eagle. Sometimes it was two boat lengths, sometimes it was a couple of feet, but everytime they tacked, the *Muskrat* closed the gap.

The *Eagle* covered all the way to weather mark. After twenty-two tacks to cover *Muskrat*, the *Eagle* rounded the weather mark three minutes and six seconds ahead. The next leg was a run followed by a beat, then another run and a final beat to the finish.

The *Eagle* had a good chute set and held starboard tack as Hoyt rounded the mark.

The *Muskrat* followed *Eagle* with another good set. The sail handling had been very good. No mistakes on either boat so far.

"Let's go ahead and jibe Hoyt. Let's see if we can get some of that lead back." They jibed right after rounding. The *Eagle* saw the move and followed suit.

"They're not goin' to leave us, Hoyt."

"Yeah, I'm not so sure they're not goin' again, Hambden."

Hoyt was right. The *Eagle* was on the move again. She was going away from the *Muskrat*. "We'd better jibe back, Hoyt."

Hambden had held the port tack for about five minutes. "Wind's hauled a little. We'll have a better angle on the other tack." They jibed and within seconds the *Eagle,* who had widened her lead, followed suit.

After about two minutes on the starboard jibe, Hoyt noticed they were catching the *Eagle.* "How do you think we're movin', Hambden?"

"We're catchin' 'em, Hoyt."

"I think you're right." The *Muskrat* was catching the *Eagle.* It was hard to understand what was happening. One minute they were real slow, the next minute they were fast.

"Don't jibe until they do, Hoyt!" Hambden wanted to hold the starboard jibe.

In about ten to twelve minutes, Bill Ficker told Davis to go for the mark. "Let's jibe her, Rod. Let's go for it." The *Eagle* jibed. Her lead had been cut down, but it was still a sizeable one.

The *Muskrat* jibed and also headed for the mark. Hambden figured they were about two minutes behind. They had closed the gap. It wasn't long before Hambden noticed another loss in speed. "We're down two knots, Hoyt."

"I know Hambden. We shouldn't be, but we are. What do you think's wrong?" Hambden looked around and could find nothing. It was very frustrating. The *Eagle* rounded four minutes ahead of *Muskrat..*

After another tacking duel up the weather leg, the gap closed again, but this time it was not as great a comeback. When they rounded the mark, they were more than three minutes behind, with one more run and then the final beat to the finish.

Both boats held on starboard tack for about two minutes. "Let's jibe, Hoyt. They've got a big lead on us. We can't just follow 'em."

Allison trimmed the main and they jibed the chute. The wind was fairly steady at about twenty-two knots.

The *Eagle* soon jibed to stay between the *Muskrat* and the marks.

"Let's go back, Hoyt." The *Muskrat* jibed again as the *Eagle* followed suit.

After jibing nine times on the last downwind leg, their positions hadn't changed.

The *Eagle* was well to the right of the rumb line, (an imaginary straight line from the weather mark to the leeward mark), so they jibed. Within a few seconds, the *Muskrat* also jibed. They were about a half mile from the last turning mark with only one leg to go. As they sailed to the mark, it was again apparent that the *Eagle* was going away from them. She had over a five minute lead. There was no way to catch her.

The *Muskrat* rounded the mark five minutes and eleven seconds behind the *Eagle*. The race was over. It would take a miracle to catch Davis now.

The crew had worked hard. No one could second guess Hambden's tactics, and Hoyt had skippered the boat well.

On the last upwind leg, the *Muskrat* again had good speed, but it was not enough to make a difference. As the *Eagle* crossed the finish line and the gun fired, her crew yelled and screamed in celebration of their victory. Four minutes and thirty seconds later, the *Muskrat* finished. Even though she had shown brilliant speed at times during the race, she was badly beaten. Four and one half minutes was considered quite a large margin in a twelve meter race.

The *Eagle* sailed close by. The entire crew stood on the weather rail and gave the *Muskrat* a wave. Rod Davis yelled, "Nice race!" to them as Hoyt waved back. It was a very nice gesture from the crew of *Eagle*, but it didn't help.

The *Muskrat* crew was very, very disappointed. It was the dream of each and every member to do well. It was to be Sam's ultimate dream come true. The *Muskrat* was the culmination of four generations of hard work for Nick and John Allen. This was a sad day indeed. All of the hopes and dreams of everyone in Oxford were shaken.

Everyone aboard the *Muskrat* had worked their hearts out. Drake, Bradley, Mark and Herbert were utterly exhausted from rowing the winches. The cockpit crew had put all they had and more into the race. Allison's arms were ready to drop off from wrestling the huge main. Schuyler and his foredeck crew performed flawlessly. It would have been much easier if there had been a major mistake made during the race. If the mainsail had ripped or the mast had been lost, they would at least have something to blame the loss on. If something had broken, they could fix it for the next race. As it stood, they had no idea why the boat didn't go off the wind. Something was seriously wrong with the *Muskrat* and no one knew what it was. The sails were lowered and properly stowed as the *Muskrat* hooked up with the *Oxford Queen* .

"What was wrong with her off the wind, Hoyt?" Sam was very much concerned.

"We don't know, Sam. She'd lose over two knots at times. It was like we'd foul on something and stop, then clear ourselves and go again."

"Let's get her back to the hoist and have a look." Hambden was anxious to see if anything was wrong with her bottom.

As they towed in, everyone gathered around the cockpit.

"I think we had to be hung up on some grass."

"I thought so too, Schuyler, but we checked. There weren't any. We kept lookin'. Weren't neither piece on her." Drake was as confused as anybody.

"I just hope it's something simple. I sure as hell hope it ain't old man Nick's design. If it's that we're through. We ain't got two or three more twelves at our dock like most the rest of'em. If our boat don't go, we do. We go home!" Hoyt was baffled.

"But, Hoyt, how can it be in the design?" Vaughn Downes said, "Shee-it, it looked like to me we was eatin' 'em up a lot of the time. It ain't like the boat changed shapes in the middle of the race."

"You're right, Vaughn. What I can't figure is why she was slow downwind. That's when we thought she'd go."

As soon as the boat was in her slip and the *Queen* was secure, Sam yelled to the crew, "We got air conditioning and the longnecks are cold. I know you guys are hot."

With the crew of the *Muskrat*, the words boys and guys always included Allison.

They gathered on the *Queen* for a cold beer, pronounced "cober" by the crew from Oxford.

"Well boys, we took a thumping today didn't we? What do you think was wrong?"

"She just died downwind, Sam. Maybe we'll find out when we haul her." Hambden said.

"I'm going to call Nick shortly. See if he has any thoughts."

"That's a good idea."

"You know, boys, the day wasn't all that bad. The boat held together well. The crew performance was excellent and the boat showed some good speed at times."

"Right, Sam." Hambden was still wondering what was wrong downwind.

They had a couple of longnecks and went over to the *Muskrat*. They hauled her out of the water. "Gawd damn, look at her, boys!" Drake walked aft toward her rudder looking at her bottom. "Ain't neither cobweb to her. She's slicker than an eel's ass."

The crew was somewhat disappointed that they found nothing wrong. It would have been easy to simply remove a large glob of seaweed from her rudder. However, they couldn't find anything. It seemed there was more than one secret with the *Muskrat* and no one knew what this one was.

"Gang, let's get these sails laid out to dry. We go against the Canadians tomorrow morning. I'm going to call Nick." Sam wandered off to make his call.

After getting the boat squared away, the crew wandered up to the P&O for a Swan or two. They gathered at their favorite table and ordered a round. No one had to help guard the boat. Sam had hired a secruity company in Perth to provide the extra manpower. The crew of *Muskrat* had plenty to worry about besides guarding the twelve. Drake questioned Sam's judgement, however.

"That's the dumbest gawd damn thing I ever heard of. Hiring a bunch of Aussies to guard the secret from another bunch of Aussies. I bet that Brewer fella owns the guard company anyway."

"You don't suppose the *Muskrat* was sabotaged do you? Somebody could have got to her last night -- especially one of them Aussie guards, and we'd never know it."

"But we didn't find nothing when we hauled her Hambden."

"Yeah, Hoyt, but come to think of it, when we went over to the *Queen* after the race, the only guards on duty was them Aussies. They could have undone what they done last night."

"You're right, Hambden. I wonder who was on duty last night. We'll have to find that out. We'd better make sure either Spry or Covey is around tonight."

At seven o'clock, Sam joined them for dinner.

"What did Nick say?" Hoyt was anxious to hear as well as the rest of the crew.

"He really didn't know, I'm sorry to report. He wants us to keep accurate time records of each leg and of each tack and jibe. He wants it for both boats in the race tomorrow. I'm not sure why."

After dinner, as they were leaving, someone yelled to Bradley from the bar. "I hear you got whipped, bunky! Now ain't that a bloody shame." It was the New Zealander, Tanker. Bradley went for him, but Drake and the crew blocked his path.

"We'll beat your little kiwi ass. You can bet on that, bunky."

Tanker made a move toward Bradley, but the two were held apart. They finally got Bradley out of the bar.

By nine thirty, everyone in the crew was back aboard the *Queen*. Their race against *True North* was at ten o'clock. It would be a busy morning.

"What did Covey say about last night, Hoyt?"

"He said that he and Spry were both off watch from four to seven. They'll be up tonight though." Everyone wondered if the newly hired guards had something to do with their defeat. They would know more after tomorrow's race.

At nine thirty, the *Muskrat* had her big main up and threw her tow line to the *Oxford Queen*. The wind was blowing about the same as the day before, around twenty-three.

"Number two, boys! Number three in the starboard locker. Nothing to port." Hambden left the port locker empty. The wind would probably increase, and if so, the number three was there. They then would put the number four in the locker, but if the wind started to decrease, it would be empty for the heavy number one.

Both Sam and John had a stopwatch to time each leg and how long each boat stayed on the port or starboard tack.

147

The ten minute gun fired.

"God, I hope she does better today."Sam was talking to John aboard the *Oxford Queen* .

"We'll soon find out."

The five minute gun fired as the *True North* reached down the line on port tack. The *Muskrat* was not more than five yards behind. The Canadian twelve eased sheets and went dead downwind. When she got close to the committee boat, the *Muskrat* followed as she very slowly jibed over to starboard and again slowly brought her hard on the wind. The *Muskrat* was directly astern about five yards away. With one minute to go, *True North* tacked over to starboard and went for the line hard on the wind.

"She's early, Hoyt! Hold port tack a few seconds before you tack. Okay! Let's go for it."

Hoyt tacked the *Muskrat* with twenty seconds to go. As usual she didn't lose any speed.

"Get her in, boys!" Hambden yelled to the men below. The jib was trimmed.

The *True North* was indeed early and she was in danger of hitting the committee boat if she reached off. Because of her position, the only thing she could do was head into the wind and ease her sails. When the gun fired, the *Muskrat* was three boat lengths, dead to weather.

Hambden and Hoyt had won the start impressively.

"Alright, *Muskrat*, let's go!" Hoyt was hyped. His boat had good speed on and the Canadians were sucking up his dirty air.

"They're going. Ready about!" Hambden saw *True North* tacking and wanted to cover.

"Nice tack boys!" Hoyt couldn't have been happier with how the twelve could tack.

Hoyt saw Hambden's signal to go again. "Ready about!

Hard alee." Again they covered the Canadian boat. Like the race with *Eagle*, *Muskrat* seemed to widen her lead on every tack.

"They're gonna give us a workout, boys!" Hambden yelled below to the men on the rowing shells.

"What's this 'gonna' shit?" Drake yelled up.

"Christ, Drake, this is only the first leg. You ain't tared yet are ya?"

"You know I ain't tared. Shee-it, them boys will run out of ocean before I git tared!"

The first leg of the race involved twenty-three tacks. As the *Muskrat* rounded the weather mark, she had an impressive fifty-seven second lead over *True North* .

The chute went up with no problems and the *Muskrat* seemed to be moving very well. The Canadian set was a little slow, but the spinnaker went up with no problem.

"We're goin' on 'em, Hoyt. Sail this thing boy!" The *Muskrat* was definitely opening her lead.

"John, she's going away from *True North* downwind. See her?"

"She sure is, Sam." John and Sam were carefully keeping track of the time. About halfway down the leg, *True North* was still following the *Muskrat* on the starboard jibe.

"Let's hold on here for a little while, Hoyt. If she jibes, we'll go too. We are solid going away from them, boys!"

About three minutes later, the *True North* jibed.

"Let's jibe, Hoyt. They've gone!"

The *Muskrat* jibed on to port tack. Hambden wanted to stay between *True North* and the leeward mark.

This was somewhat of an unusual downwind leg. The boats each jibed only once. John and Sam made note of the time of the jibe. Then it happened again. "She's stopped again,

Hoyt! Gawd damn boat's dead in the water!"

The *Muskrat* lost almost three knots. Things had been going so well. It was almost more than they could take. *True North* beat them to the leeward mark by twelve seconds after the *Muskrat* had built such an impressive lead.

That was it for the day. They never caught the Canadians again. There was a problem with the *Muskrat* and unfortunately the problem was serious and nobody understood what it was. The only thing they knew was that all of a sudden the boat stopped off the wind.

Sam was devastated. It took all the patience he could muster to follow the boat for the rest of the race. To say the least, it was pure misery for Hoyt and the crew to finish all eight legs of the course, knowing the boat would stop at some point in every reach and every run. To their credit, however, they gave it one hundred and fifty percent all the way. Their sail handling was excellent and their tacks were crisp, but it wasn't close. *True North* won by seven minutes and eighteen seconds.

The tow back to Fishing Boat Harbor was long and quiet. When the boats were tied up, Sam came over to the *Muskrat*. "Long day, eh boys?"

"We ain't licked yet, gawd damn it. Hoyt was trying to keep everyone's spirits up even though his were about as low as they could be. "Ain't neither person on *Muskrat* been quitters. Ain't nothin' wrong 'bout losing the first two races down here. I just don't want to lose the last one!"

Sam was also low. He agreed, nobody on the *Muskrat* was a quitter, but the boat did have a very serious problem. He spoke to the crew. "Tomorrow we are scheduled to race *New Zealand*. She is a proven boat. She was second in the Worlds behind *Australia III*. She whipped every American challenger there.

"I think we should do two things. I think we should take a lay day, (The boats had the option to postpone a race for a day.) and I think I should get old man Nick down here."

"Good idea, Sam." Hoyt agreed, "If anybody can figure this out, it's Nick."

Sam called Nick and made the necessary arrangements for Nick to fly to Perth. Nick was not receptive to the idea, to say the least. Nick's idea of traveling was going over to Brinkley's for an ice cream cone. However, Sam had quite a bit of leverage, about one-and-a-half million dollars worth. He arranged for a quick passport and Nick was on his way to Australia early the next morning. Sam also called the Royal Perth Yacht Club and asked for a lay day. The "Kiwis" would have to wait for their race against the *Muskrat*.

The entire crew was down as they went to the P&O for a couple of tinnies. As they sat around the table, they tried to figure what had happened to the boat on the downwind legs. No one could figure what could possibly be the problem. They all looked forward to Nick's arrival, hoping he would get there before the next race, which was scheduled for Wednesday at noon. Three defeats in a row would be too much. Especially at the hands of *New Zealand*.

At about eight o'clock, their dinners were served in the bar. They noticed some activity over at the arm wrestling table. Some people gathered around to watch the beginning of the arm wrestling tournament. Tonight started the first round.

Thirty-two teams had signed up. There would be a series of four eliminations, each one eliminating half of the teams. After the fourth series, there would be only two teams left to wrestle for the championship and the five thousand dollars.

There were two people on each team. If, after wrestling an opponent, one teammate won and one lost, the two winners would wrestle to break the tie.

Bradley and Drake looked around, but didn't see anybody they recognized. "I wonder if Tanker is in this thing, Bradley."

"I'll bet he is, Drake." There was a long pause as Bradley leaned over toward Drake. "You don't suppose Blackdog is in this thing do ya?"

"I ain't so sure you'd recognize him after what I did to him. I know you'd never recognize his buddy."

"I can tell you one thing, Drake." Bradley was now whispering in Drake's ear and his hand covered a portion of his mouth. "I'm afraid they'll recognize us, and when they do, there's gonna be trouble."

"You got that right, Bradley."

Sam had been watching the arm wrestling matches behind him and had also noticed Drake and Bradley whispering in each other's ear. He became a little suspicious. "Somebody said this is an arm wrestling contest. Is that right, boys?" He looked straight across the table at Drake and Bradley.

"I think so, Sam. I'm not sure, but I think there's two men on a team." Drake was trying to play dumb.

"You boys aren't considering signing up for it are you?"

"Oh no. We wouldn't be interested in that!" Bradley was lying through his teeth. Their first round was scheduled for eleven o'clock the next night. If Sam knew about it, he'd have a stroke; especially with a race against *New Zealand* the next morning.

Sam and the crew watched several matches. Some of the men who were participating were huge, with big bulging muscles nearly ripping the short sleeves of their shirts. Each team seemed to have its own cheering section. At the conclusion of every match, there were loud screams of excitement and a call for another "shout" or round of beer.

152

Drake and Bradley enjoyed watching. After seeing some of their competition, they knew their work was going to be cut out for them. That five thousand dollar prize was going to be tough to get.

At midnight everyone went back to the boat. Sam had left earlier for his hotel. They were greeted at the gate by three of the Aussie guards. The crew still questioned Sam hiring the Australians.

It was almost ten in the morning by the time all the crew got going for the day. There was nothing to do on the boat and no race scheduled until the next day, so they took that opportunity to sack in.

Using the *Oxford Queen* as their hotel was working out well. Allison slept in the forepeak where she had her own head and a comfortable "V" berth. Just aft of the fore peak was a cabin with four bunks, an upper and a lower on each side. That's where all four of the "rowers" bunked. They were comfortable there except for some initial snoring problems.

Herbert Loscomb was a very loud snorer and had kept Mark Litty up the entire first night they were aboard. Herbert was snoring so loud he made the brass hatch above his bunk rattle. He would snore and then, when he exhaled, he would gag. He gagged so much Mark thought he was going to choke to death. At about four that morning, Mark was so tired he hoped Herbert *would* choke to death so he could get some sleep.

They figured out how to solve the problem, however. The bunks they were sleeping on were pipe berths. They hung from the ceiling by two pieces of rope which ran through two blocks and tied to a cleat on the forward bulkhead. The outboard side of the bunk was hinged to the hull. If the boat was heeled over or was rolling, you could adjust the rope so that your bunk was at any angle you preferred.

After the first night, whenever Herbert snored, Mark would simply undo the rope and change the angle of Herbert's bunk. If it got too bad, he'd either untie the rope and pull Herbert real hard, mashing him against the hull, or he'd simply untie the rope and let Herbert go flying to the floor. It didn't take long for him to realize that the snoring had to stop.

The main cabin was aft of Herbert and the boys. This was more of a living area with a sofa and several chairs. On one side was a small galley which was very convenient for snacks and coffee. The refrigerator was always well stocked with Budweiser longnecks. There was a large supply hidden in the *Queens's* bilge.

Aft of the main salon were two more cabins each sleeping four. Sky, Jimmy, Vaughn and Glenn shared the first, and Hoyt, Hambden, Bailey and Pete slept in the cabin all the way aft.

Each of the three cabins had a small head with a shower. Above the main salon was the wheel house. Below decks was storage and, of course, the engine room.

All of the sailing gear that had come over on the *Queen* had been taken ashore and put in the shed.

As far as Spry and Covey's sleeping arrangements, they slept on the *Muskrat* for security reasons.

The *Oxford Queen* was very comfortable. The crew seemed happy staying aboard. After all, they were sailors. Why not stay on a boat, and a good old Oxford buy boat at that.

The crew met at the P&O at about noon for lunch. They had coffee and donuts on board for their morning snack. When they entered the hotel, they learned of more trouble. There had been an attempted break-in of the Italian compound last night. Someone had tried to get to the *Azzura*. This time they came by water. Scuba divers came into the harbor around two o'clock.

Nobody knows how many men were involved or where else they went. Luckily, one of the guards was at the end of the dock and noticed the bubbles coming from the airtanks. He ordered the flood lights turned on. The bubbles then turned away and headed out toward the mouth of the harbor. The guard thought he made out what looked to be the outlines of at least two divers, but they were fairly deep, and the lights reflecting on the water made it hard to tell. The police were called, but by the time they could get divers overboard, it was too late.

This, of course, caused the crew of the *Muskrat* concern. Those divers could have already investigated their compound.

"I doubt it, Bradley. Keep in mind, we have our electric netting around her. She also is hauled out . If anyone were to take pictures, someone would have seen the flash."

"I hope you're right, Hambden." Drake spoke up. "I hope every gawd damn sailin' team here gits pictures of her bottom and copies every inch of her. We'd be smart to take the pictures and pass 'em out ourselves. Shee-it! My daddy's *Eel's* faster than she'll ever be!"

"Shut up, Drake! Don't you go talkin' like that."

Drake was mumbling to himself. "Come halfway round the world to race in the America's Cup, and I'm on the only twelve meter that's a row boat. Big deal! Spend all my winter rowin'."

"Oh shut up, Drake!"

There were no other reports of anyone seeing the divers from any of the other compounds.

After lunch the crew headed back to the compound to meet Sam and they told him of the *Azzura* incident.

"When did you say Nick is arriving, Sam?" Hambden really was anxious for Nick to see if he could figure out the problem.

"I'm not sure, Hambden. I told Pucky Lappen at the travel

agency to get him here as soon as humanly possible. She said she would. I guess that could be tonight at the earliest. I'll bet Pucky will have her hands full getting old man Nick on a plane."

The crew did a little maintenance work on the boat. They took some of the winches apart and greased them. They went over the rowing machine and sent Sky aloft to check on the blocks, etc.

After two or three hours working on the boat, they wandered around the harbor for awhile and as usual ended up back at the P&O bar. The old hotel was really home to them. They all had become good friends with the bartender and waitress who did their best to keep the *Muskrat* crew's favorite table available for them. The crew constantly teased them about not serving Bud longnecks. The bartender called a can of Swan "our Freo short necks."

Sam joined them for dinner at eight. They all had a lovely steak which was the special of the night, and at around ten o'clock, Sam suggested the crew get back to the boat. It would be an early morning with a ten o'clock start scheduled. Sam went back to his hotel as the crew headed for the harbor.

Bradley and Draked doubled back to the P&O. They had their match scheduled for eleven.

After ordering a tinnie, they watched the match just prior to theirs. The men who competed were huge, each weighing at least two-fifteen. One team was from Perth and the other team was from Sidney.

The match was a draw after each team suffered a loss. The two winners faced each other at the table as the referee made sure their grips were fair. The man from Sidney looked his opponent in the eye and said, "Get ready to go down, Sandgroper." That is a name given to the Aussies who live in Perth.

From the expression on the Perth man's face, the name was not appreciated.

The whistle blew and before he knew it, the sand groper had whipped the boy from Sidney. A huge round of applause swept through the bar.

The winner looked at this victim and said, "Well now, myte, you can grope your fat ass back to Sidney, now can't you?"

As Drake and Bradley stepped up to the table, they were met by their opponents. They were also from Perth, and seemed very nice. They shook hands and wished each other luck. These were typical Aussies. One of them was about six foot three inches and weighed two hundred and ten pounds, and introduced himself as Jason. The other was very short, around five-eight and stocky, weighing around one hundred eighty. His name was Curt.

Bradley went against Jason first. The referee checked the grips and the whistle blew.

Jason got the initial edge and had Bradley's arm about half way down. With a concerted effort, Bradley got his arm back to the starting position. They stayed there for at least ten seconds, neither able to budge the other. As they were locked in the upright position, Bradley's eyes wandered for a second. Out of the corner of his eye, he recognized Tanker standing not more than ten feet from him in the crowd.

"Come on, Bradley!" Drake was rooting him on.

Slowly, Bradley brought Jason's arm down. He had him within six inches of a pin when Jason fought back. As the arms got closer to the upright position, Bradley gave it his best rush of power. It was too much for Jason. He went down for the pin.

Bradley had won the match. It almost seemed as though Bradley was the hometown boy as he got a loud round of applause. The *Muskrat* crew seemed to be well liked in Freo.

There was one person who was not clapping however. Tanker just stared at Bradley with a very disagreeable expression on his face. Tanker couldn't stand to see Bradley win without making a smart comment.

"Well, at least you can win at something, Myte! Maybe you should stay here tomorrow!"

Bradley walked over to Tanker and pointed his finger in his face. "You keep mouthin' off and you'll spend tomorrow in the hospital, smart ass!"

The bartender yelled at them to knock it off and surprisingly enough, they did.

"Come on, Drake! Let's go, boy!" Bradley turned his attention back to the match as Drake gripped the hand of Curt. The ref again checked the grips of both men to make sure neither had the advantage. As he raised both of his hands, he blew the whistle, signaling the match to begin.

Before Drake knew what had hit him, he had been pinned. It seemed over before it had started. Drake couldn't believe it. He was stunned.

The referee motioned for Bradley to return to the table to break the tie. He went up and faced the five-ten Curt gripping his hand to begin the match.

"Watch him, Bradley. Watch him at the whistle!" Drake warned his partner.

The whistle blew, and this time Bradley held his ground. Curt moved Bradley's arm a little toward the mat, but only a couple of inches. After the initial movement, it was Bradley who was in control. He slowly, but surely, sent Curt's arm toward the table top. His strength was too much. He soon pinned his opponent.

"Way to go, Bradley!" Drake joined the crowd in applauding Bradley's victory.

Tanker again had something to say, this time to Drake. "You let that little runt whip you, myte?"

That was it. Drake lunged at Tanker throwing a solid right to his chin. Tanker was unbelievably strong. He grabbed Drake's shirt with his left hand and slammed a wooden chair over his head. The chair burst into a hundred pieces. It didn't phase Drake a bit. He popped Tanker with another strong right and tagged him on the right eye. Bradley had made his way across the room, knocking several people down on the way. Right behind him was the "runt" Curt who was mad as anybody at Tanker.

Bradley stung Tanker with a right and caught him in his left eye. Curt bulldozed into Tanker, driving his head into Tanker's stomach, throwing him back against the bar. Curt threw a left and hit him in the right eye. It seemed every punch landed in one of Tanker's eyes. He grabbed Curt and literally threw him across the bar room. Curt landed on a table and rolled it over spilling him in the laps of several people.

Drake was face to face with Tanker with his right hand cocked, ready to throw another blow. Tanker grabbed his right arm and then his left. With all his might, he pulled Drake toward him as he lowered his big bald head. There was a loud crunch as Tanker's head caught Drake's nose. Blood flew everywhere.

Just then a whistle blew. This time it was not an arm wrestling match starting. It was the police.

Tanker saw the cops and took off through the crowd toward the far corner. He was heading away from the door toward a small stained-glass window which was about five feet off the floor. Tanker extended his arms and dove through. He disappeared as thousands of tiny multi-colored pieces of glass flew everywhere.

At six the next morning, Samuel E. Johnson III was awakened by a phone call.

"Mr. Johnson?"

"Yes, this is Sam Johnson. What is it?"

"Mr. Johnson, this is the Fremantle Police Department!"

"Someone got into our compound! Did you catch them? I hope you got 'em!"

"No sir. Well, yes and no".

"Spit it out, boy! Tell me something!"

"Well, no. Nobody broke into your compound, but yes we caught 'em."

"I don't understand!"

"We've got two of your crew down here at the jail, sir. We got them last night, fighting at the P&O Hotel bar. If you want to get 'em out, you'll have to come down here and pay their fine and sign some papers. Of course, if you want me to put 'em up for a few more nights, we've got two vacancies. The food ain't much, but they won't get into any bar room brawls, I can promise you that, myte."

"God damn those boys! I'll never guess which two you have. Are their names Drake and Bradley?"

"That's right , myte."

"I'll be down as soon as I get some clothes on."

"Suit yourself, myte."

Sam was mad as hell. He had plenty to worry about besides two men acting like kids. If there wasn't a race scheduled that day, he sure as hell would have left them in jail as long as he could. Their behavior was a real problem. Sam thought that it was going to be just a matter time before that pair got into more serious trouble.

Drake and Bradley woke up in their cell with Curt.

"That big son-of-a-bitch got away last night didn't he,

Drake?"

"I'm afraid so, Bradley. You alright, Curt?"

"I think so, myte. I'd like to have another go at that Tanker chap though."

"I'm sure we will. I ain't looking forward to seein' Sam, I can tell you that."

"Who's Sam, myte?

"He's the owner of our boat, the *Muskrat*. He'll most likely be down to git us out'a here. You got anybody comin' to git you out, old buddy?"

"Jason will be down shortly, I'm sure."

Sam arrived at seven o'clock. He paid the fines, signed the papers and bailed the boys out of jail. He was very unhappy. "God damn you two! What the hell is going on? The last time I saw you, you were headed down to the boat. What happened?"

"Um-um," Bradley didn't know how much Sam knew. "We ah—we went back to git my wallet. I lost my wallet."

"Since when is it against the law to get your wallet, Bradley? God damn it! Tell me what happened."

"Well ah—when we got back to the bar this great big guy from New Zealand started a fight with this real little fella and we didn't think it was fair."

"So you got into the fight too? That's real good, boys. You showed lots of smarts. You sure it didn't have something to do with the arm wrestling contest?"

"Oh no, Sam. No indeedy."

"I'm tempted to put you two on the next plane back to the states. You're nothing but trouble. Drake, we've been in two races and you've been in jail three times. I want to tell you something, Drake. You're gonna to be eliminated long before the *Muskrat* is.

161

Chapter Eight

They went straight to the compound to get ready for the race. Bradley and Drake were afraid to say anything. They wondered if Old Man Nick had arrived but weren't about to ask Sam.

As they got aboard the *Muskrat*, Hoyt asked Drake where he and Bradley had been. Drake lowered his head like a little kid with his hand caught in the cookie jar.

"In jail again, Hoyt. We got in another fight at the hotel last night. That gawd damn kiwi Tanker, I'd like to kill him!"

"He'll be on the *New Zealand* today racin' against us."

"I know. Hoyt, we gotta beat that bastard today. We just gotta."

Drake's eyes got real big as he asked, "Is Nick here? Did he come in last night?"

"Afraid not, Drake."

"Shee-it!" Drake was really disappointed. He felt there was no way they could beat the *New Zealand* without him. The *New Zealand* had already won over *Azzurra*.

At ten thirty, there was still no word from Nick.

"We'll wait another ten minutes and then we've got to go." Sam was as anxious as anyone for Nick to arrive.

At eleven o'clock, the *Queen* headed out of Fishing Boat Harbor with the *Muskrat* in tow. As they passed America's Cup Harbor, they saw the *New Zealand* being towed out through the breakwaters. She was a good-looking twelve designed by Ron Holland, Bruce Farr and Laurie Davidson. She was skippered by the youngest helmsman of all the twelves, Chris Dickson. The *New Zealand* was made of fiberglass and was known as the "Plastic Fantastic." The kiwis were used to the heavy weather sailing, and it was blowing a steady twenty-five.

Bradley and Drake looked to see if Tanker was aboard, but they were too far away.

As they got closer to the starting line, Hambden noticed a very confused sea. The waves were bigger than normal and had no pattern at all. Hambden felt this would be to their advantage, since he'd never seen any fiberglass as light as ruddynut. He wished Nick was with them.

When the *Queen* throttled down and headed around into the wind, Hoyt called for the main. After the main was hoisted, Hambden yelled to the crew. It was hard to hear over the main flapping in the twenty-five knot breeze. "Number two on deck ready to fire. Number three in the starboard locker. Nothin' to port."

When the headsails were in place, Hoyt asked Hambden if they were ready to leave the *Queen* .

"I guess so, Hoyt. We got everything we need from the tender, boys?"

"We got everything, Hambden. We even brought a little extra." Glenn yelled from below.

"What does he mean, Hambden?"

"Beats me, let's get goin'. Let off the tow line, Sky!"

Hambden thought to himself. He was going to be real aggressive the entire race. He had to go all out today. They hadn't won a race. He thought about his tactics at the start.

Sky had undone the tow line and was ready to heave it back

to the *Queen* . Just then John Dryden yelled.

"No, Sky! Stop! Tie her back up."

No one aboard the *Muskrat* knew what was going on.

"What's wrong up there, Sky? What did John say?"

"Beats the shit out'a me, Hoyt!" Hambden looked at his watch. "Only three minutes to the first gun. What the hell's goin' on up there?"

The tender was towing them away from the line leaving them with a dead downwind sail to their start.

"We're gonna be in trouble, Sky. We're gonna be late! Find out what the hell's goin' on!"

Both John and Sam were looking through binoculars back toward the Harbor.

"What the hell are they lookin' at?" Hoyt was getting real concerned.

"Hambden, take the wheel." Hoyt went forward.

"John! Sam! What are you lookin' at? We're late for the start!"

"Hang on, Hoyt." Sam didn't say what they saw.

Sam said something to John and John put down his glasses and ran below. In just a few seconds, he appeared again with a legal pad. By now the rower's heads were up looking over the after cockpit trying to see what the problem was. Drake saw John hand the pad of paper to Sam. "I guess they're goin' to take notes of us missin' the start, Hambden."

"Shut up, Drake! Git below, damn it!"

There were fifteen seconds to the first gun.

"Cut us loose, Hoyt. I don't care what they say. Cut this gawd damn boat loose!"

Just then the crew saw a lovely sight pop from behind one of the big rolling seas. It was an Avon dinghy with a very young boy at the handle of the outboard. There was only one other passenger in the boat. It was none other than old man Nick Benson straight from Oxford, Maryland.

The crew was ecstatic, especially Hambden. "Git your ass on here, Nick! Gawd damn if we ain't happy to see you Cap'n." Nick had just arrived in Freo and had hired the kid and the dinghy to get him to the line. They didn't have a second to spare. The *Queen* backed down and Sam handed Sky the pad of paper. It contained the times recorded on the second race.

"Help Nick aboard, Drake!"

"Gawd damn it, Hoyt. Hang on to your binnacle. I don't want to hurt him. He's older'n dirt!" Drake helped Nick aboard and the tow line was released.

"Fire up the jib! Gawd damn, Nick, where the hell have you been?" Hoyt asked him, "at the P&O having a tinnie or two?

"I don't know nothin' about no P&O or tinnie, but I do know that if that's the ten-minute signal flyin,' we're in trouble."

The *New Zealand* had its sails up and was near the committee boat. They were upwind of the start and Hambden didn't hear the gun. He had no idea how long it had been since it fired.

"Git the ounce and a half up here. Let's set the chute." Within two minutes, the spinnaker was flying. The *Muskrat* was desperately trying to get back for the start.

"Drop the jib down halfway," Hambden yelled to the foredeck.

Hambden saw the smoke of the five-minute gun as he started his watch.

"Five minutes to start! Keep that chute drawin', Bailey. Hawk that main, Allison. It's gonna be close."

New Zealand didn't know what was going on. They were just reaching up and down the line as they watched the *Muskrat* screaming down to the line, surfing off the seas. "Quite an unusual starting tactic isn't it, Chris?" the tactician on the kiwi boat asked Chris Dickson, the skipper.

"Maybe they started early and they're on their second leg, myte!" Chris jokingly added. He didn't really take the *Muskrat* seriously. He had seen her unusual rig and sails and, of course, knew of her two losses. As far as he was concerned, if he could keep his mast in the boat, he could simply sail the course and win.

As the *Muskrat* ran for the line on starboard, Old Man Nick Benson studied the notes Sam and John had taken. He was in the cockpit with Hoyt, trying to stay out of his way. "The extra weight aboard wouldn't hurt in this air," he thought to himself.

"Them notes mean anything, Nick?"

"I think they do, Glenn. I should know after the second leg. I'll know for sure after the reaching leg."

"Fifteen seconds to shape down, Hoyt. One minute fifteen seconds to gun!" Hambden yelled to Hoyt.

"Are we going to make it, Hambden?"

"It's gonna be close. Jib up with lots of halyard tension." They were surfing down to the line with forty seconds to the gun.

"We'll douse the chute and harden up when we get there. Twenty seconds." Hambden knew they wouldn't make it.

The kiwi boat was trimming in and going for the start. They were on port tack, moving well. As the gun sounded, they were right on the line. *Muskrat* still had her chute as she surfed off a big wave about six boat lengths away. It was the most unusual start that the race committee and the spectators had ever seen; the *New Zealand* hard on the wind going for the starting line and the *Muskrat* going dead downwind towards her on the wrong side of the line. As the *New Zealand* passed the *Muskrat*, they were within twenty feet of each other; the kiwi boat hard on the wind, the *Muskrat* under spinnaker.

"Rather unusual, myte!" Dickson said to his tactician.

Drake and Bradley heard a familiar voice from the *New Zealand.* "Nice start bunky!"

Both Bradley and Drake jumped off their machines and appeared in the aft cockpit. As they looked over at the other boat, they saw Tanker not more than thirty feet away. "Hey, Drake, they got a raccoon on the boat. Look, our little bunky's a raccoon!"

Tanker had two of the blackest eyes they had ever seen. He did look like a raccoon. Tanker yelled back, "I said you should have stayed at the bar." Bradley and Drake would have given anything to get their hands on him.

"Git the hell below!" Hambden was having a fit. "Chute down! Drop it! Get ready to harden up, Hoyt. It'll be a big trim, Allison, use the grinders! Okay, we're clear."

The number two and the main were trimmed and they finally were on the weather leg on starboard tack. As soon as they headed up, the *New Zealand* tacked over to cover. They were a quarter of a mile ahead. Even though she was hobby-horsing quite a bit, they seemed to be moving well.

"We got to tack, Hoyt. Let's see if they'll cover."

"Ready about! Hard alee!"

Nick was tickled with the way the *Muskrat* went about. His rowing grinders worked perfectly.

The *New Zealand* covered.

"How do you think she's movin', Nick?"

"She's doin' alright, Hoyt. I'm worried about her downwind though."

"Tell us about it!" Nobody was worried about the downwind legs more than Hoyt.

"Too bad we got the start we did, Nick." Drake piped up from below," If you'd gotten an earlier flight, we'd be round the mark now." Drake wasn't far from being right. They had given away nearly ten minutes.

The *Muskrat* tacked eighteen times on the first leg. She closed the *New Zealand* lead by nearly two minutes. The boat moved to weather faster than any they had raced.

The kiwis rounded the weather mark eight minutes fifteen seconds ahead. Their spinnaker set was sloppy and cost them a little time. The set on the *Muskrat* was perfect. Nick got a kick out of seeing how fast the chute went up.

"Now, Nick, I don't know why, but on our first two races she stopped downwind. Do you have any theories?" Hambden was praying Nick could figure out something.

"Not yet, Hambden, but I'd go right for the mark on this leg. Stay on starboard as long as you can."

The *New Zealand* was sailing at a much faster angle. They too were on starboard tack, but Chris Dickson was holding up a little.

"She's slow at this angle, Nick. Can't Hoyt hold her up some?"

"I'd go right for the mark, Hambden."

"But she's slow as shit. We're almost by the lee, Nick."

Nick had been up for over twenty four hours and his nerves were on edge. He didn't want to come in the first place. One thing he didn't want to do was argue with anybody. "Hambden, you listen to me. Look at my lips, boy! You've raced two races. You've lost twice. If my arithmetic is right, two minus two is zero. You have won zero races. Now Sam had me come halfway 'round the world to see if I could help git rid of the zero. I'm here, see? This is me! I'm Nick. I'm here to help you. Now, I say go for the mark. Read my lips, Hambden. GO FOR THE MARK!"

"I'm sorry, Nick. I just want to whip them boys so bad."

Drake yelled up from below, "Hambden, I think if Nick had his choice, he'd just as soon go for the mark!"

"Shut up, Drake!" Hambden looked below at the rowers. "What the shit have you got in your hand, Drake?"

"What the shit does it look like? It's a longneck."

The grinders had decided they needed a beer or two on the downwind leg just like they did back on the Chesapeake Bay. That was what Glenn meant by the "little extra" they had gotten from the tender. They didn't see how it could slow them up any. Nestled between the rowing machines was a plastic cooler filled with shaved ice and Budweiser longnecks. They looked good to Hambden. They looked like home. Why not have a few aboard.

"Give me one, Drake! Want a beer, Hoyt?"

"Hell yes!"

"You boys forward want a quick beer before we git to the mark? We ain't jibing. I'm pretty sure about that!"

The crew had a round of longnecks on the downwind leg. Everyone had a beer in their hand, and it finally felt like they were racing a sailboat.

As they rounded the leeward mark, they were six minutes behind the *New Zealand* .

"We picked up over two minutes on her boys. On a downwind leg! Yah-hoo!"

The crew was ecstatic. "How did we do it, Nick?" Hambden had no idea how they caught them.

Drake yelled from below, "It's the longnecks!" The entire crew agreed just for laughs. They did seem more relaxed.

"Hambden, I was studying them times from the race against the Canadian boat." Nick was telling Hoyt and Hambden, "The boat was fast on every weather leg and half of every reach and run."

"What do you mean by half, Nick?" Drake couldn't resist: "Hambden, if you have two apples and you take away one, that's half!"

"Shut up, Drake!"

Nick continued, "Everytime this boat was on port tack downwind, she'd slow down. She was fast on starboard on the same leg. It's just port she's slow!"

"She was?"

"Yes, she was. That's why I didn't want to jibe on the last leg. Now we've got to get goin' on this weather leg. *New Zealand's* still over six minutes ahead and we will probably git creamed on the second reaching leg. Ain't neither thing we can do about it either. It's a port reach period."

Back aboard the *Queen*, Sam and John were going crazy. For the first time they saw the *Muskrat* do well on a downwind leg. "I don't know what Nick did, but I could kiss him!" Sam was thrilled. "Now come on, boys, let's get 'em. We're on the wind!"

They were six minutes, ten seconds behind at the leeward mark. Over four minutes had been wiped off the ten minutes they lost at the start. However, they had a port tack reach they were stuck with, and if the wind hauled any to the east, their runs would be on port tack, too.

"Ready about! Hard alee!" The *Muskrat* tacked for the tenth time. Each tack brought them a little closer to the *New Zealand* .

"If Nick had only caught a flight out of BWI two minutes earlier," Drake thought to himself.

By the time the *Muskrat* reached the weather mark, she was four minutes three seconds behind. They had closed the lead again.

They rounded the weather mark and popped out the reaching chute. The wind was building slightly gusting to twenty-eight. The spinnaker set was perfect again. The boys from Oxford knew how to handle the sails. The *Muskrat* surfed toward the mark, flying as she came off the big seas. She seemed to be gaining on the kiwis with every wave. Allison worked the main in and out. At times, the wind was too much for Hoyt and he called for an ease. Even though she had help with the grinders below, she was exhausted as they prepared to jibe around the mark.

The *New Zealand* jibed at the mark. She was three minutes and forty-five seconds ahead. The *Muskrat* did the leg eighteen seconds faster than the New Zealanders. She jibed and went on the port tack.

"We'll take a beatin' now, boys!" Nick warned Hambden as he went below to see if he could find the problem.

"She's dead, Nick. We've lost our speed again. See anything down there?" Hambden was beside himself again.

"Not yet, Hambden."

The boat had stopped. There was absolutely nothing they could do. Drake looked at Bradley. "Let's have a beer, Bradley."

"Good idea, Drake."

The rowing grinders had a longneck.

"We'll need the vitamins for the weather leg," Drake said to Bradley.

The *Muskrat* took a terrible beating on the reaching leg. As hard as Hoyt worked to get the boat going, she just wouldn't get out of her own way. They finally got to the leeward mark eight minutes thirteen seconds behind. Almost four and one half minutes were lost on the leg.

There were only three legs to go; two on the wind and one run. It would be nearly impossible to catch the *New Zealand*.

Sam and John could barely maintain their sanity through the second reaching leg. They were relieved to see the *Muskrat* back on the wind.

They decided to stay with the number two, but it was very close to its limit. The wind was hitting thirty in the gusts. The *New Zealand* also had her number two. The jib was full of water most of the time, and she was losing ground to the *Muskrat* . The Oxford boys tacked every couple of minutes and the boys below really got a workout.

"Keep it up down there, boys. We're gainin' on 'em!" Nick gave the rowing grinders some encouragement. They had tacked twelve times on the leg and they were only halfway there. Schuyler was looking ahead at the *New Zealand*.

"We're gittin' her, Hoyt. Little by little, we're closin'."

Suddenly, Sky yelled, "She's blown her headsail! Look, she's ripped her jib! Hot damn, Hoyt, look! Look!"

The *New Zealand* was in trouble. The foot of her number two couldn't take the big seas and had ripped. The tear was about halfway between the tack and clew and went straight up through three panels. She just sat there hobby-horsing under main alone as the crew brought up the number three. Hambden didn't want to take any chances.

"Let's go to our number three, boys. Let's play it safe. It took less than a minute to make the change. "Number two back in the starboard locker. Put the number four in the port just to be safe. Nice work, gang!"

The *Muskrat* had changed jibs before the *New Zealand* could change hers. Nick's system was truly ingenious. The blown out sail had been very costly to the *New Zealand*. As the *Muskrat* rounded the weather mark, she was less than three minutes behind. Both boats had good spinnaker sets.

"Go for the mark, Hoyt." Nick wanted to stay on starboard

tack. "If you get let down, go with it. Put some money in the bank."

The *New Zealand* held down with the *Muskrat* staying between her and the mark. She was holding her own.

"Are we catchin' her, Hambden?" Hoyt looked at his stadometer.

"No. We're stayin' even." Nick wasn't surprised. He had an idea of what the problem was.

"That's the best we can do now, boys." The wind had hauled very slightly to the east. They were sailing by the lee at times. It was very tricky steering. Hoyt was constantly having to spin the wheel as the boat rolled relentlessly. Her spinnaker pole looked like it would hit the water when they rolled to weather.

"Hang in there, Hoyt!" Nick knew he had his hands full.

"We're gainin' a little now. Drive her, boy!" Hambden noticed they were closing the gap. He thought about rounding. "This is going to be a little tricky at the mark. Now listen to me. We're going to try somethin' we ain't done before. We've got to gamble now. We can win or lose this race at this mark. We'll carry the chute on starboard right to the buoy. We set the number three at the last second. Put the halyard in high gear with the rowers. The jib will be on the starboard side just ahead of the pole.

"Now here's the tricky part. Listen up. Trip the chute out of the pole. Sky, you pull the topping lift as hard as you can while Jimmy eases the foreguy. Make damn sure that foreguy is eased."

The crew was somewhat confused. The usual procedure was to hoist the jib up on the port side, drop the pole on deck and get rid of the topping lift, then jibe over and trim. Hambden continued: "By pulling on the topping lift, the pole

173

will go up against the mast and be out of the way so the jib can be trimmed. The chute has to be dropped quickly. Just let it go. We'll get it in, understand?"

It made sense. By doing this maneuver, they didn't have to jibe over to port until they actually rounded the mark. It also enabled them to carry the chute to the mark. It was a gamble, but they couldn't afford any loss of speed now. There was only one leg to go.

They were very close to the mark. A lot would be riding on this maneuver. "Allison, as the jib goes up start trimming the main. Everyone has to do their job together. This has to be one slow jibe with the jib going up and the chute down as we perform it. Make damn sure that jib sheet is under the foreguy. We'll have to put the weather sheet on later."

The *New Zealand* approached the mark with her pole to port. She had hardened up on starboard tack and jibed over. The *Muskrat* couldn't afford that luxury. They couldn't go downwind on the port tack.

The kiwis rounded the mark. "They're not far ahead of us boys. We've caught her. If we can pull this off, we'll have a good shot at her on the last leg."

Sam was beside himself back on the *Queen*. They were right below the leeward mark; not fifty yards away.

"What in the world are they going to do, John? They've left no room to jibe."

"They're goin' to be in a heap of trouble, Sam. I can't figure it. After playin' catch-up all day, they must have somethin' up their sleeve."

"I've never seen a boat in that position at the mark stay out of trouble."

The *Muskrat* was very close to the mark.

"You, boys, ready below? First the jib up, trip chute, pole

up, jibe and trim on the wind. You ready, Allison? Sky, is the jib ready?"

"It's ready, Hambden."

"Pull like hell on that topping lift when it's time, Sky. Jimmy, lots of ease on the foreguy. Trim the main, Allison! Jib up!" Hambden screamed his orders. They were at the mark. The jib flew up the headstay. "Just a little sheet on that jib! Trip the chute!"

The afterguy popped out of the pole, but there was a problem. The pole was under the afterguy and Sky couldn't raise it.

"The pole's under the afterguy, Hoyt! I can't get it up!"

If they jibed with the pole to starboard, it would be under water. The boat would stop until the pole either was cleared or broke. They were in a jam. Something had to be done and done right now, Hoyt thought to himself. He was a great helmsman. He had a clear picture of the problem and had an idea.

He sailed to port slightly sailing by the lee. The boat rolled to port and then to starboard, the pole almost in the water. This made the chute drift to the right, beyond the spinnaker pole.

"Now, Sky! Pull now!" The pole cleared. "Chute down!" They were out of the jam.

They were overlapped with the buoy. The chute came down nicely, and Hoyt threw the wheel over.

"Trim! Trim! Trim!"

The *Muskrat* rolled over to port tack as she came off a big sea. She swung around the leeward mark, missing it by inches. The main and jib trimmed in perfectly; the chute was stowed below and on board the *Muskrat* were the proudest skipper, builder and crew ever to round a leeward mark.

Hambden's scheme had worked. They had nearly caught the *New Zealand*. She was only four boat lengths ahead.

Sam and John Dryden were speechless during the rounding. They couldn't believe what they had seen. They both stood at the rail outside of the wheelhouse. Covey was driving the boat and Spry was with him in the wheelhouse.

As the twelves started their final beat to weather, Sam didn't say a word to John. He turned around to Spry. "Git us two strong bourbons, Spry. My nerves are shot!"

Both boats were pounding in the seas; the *New Zealand* hobby-horsing more than the *Muskrat.*

"Ready about!' Hoyt had gotten the signal from Hambden.

"Hard alee!" Hoyt went over to starboard tack. The boat came around smartly.

New Zealand covered, losing about a quarter of a boat length.

Hambden yelled below, "Everything alright, boys? You got a few tacks in ya? This is the last leg. We're closin' on them kiwis!"

"Don't just stand there, Hambden. Tack the damn boat!" Drake wanted to whip that boat more than anybody. He kept thinking of his friend, Tanker, when he was rowing the machine.

"Ready about! Hard alee!" They rolled her over to port. The kiwis covered as usual. The distance between the two was getting shorter.

"Let's go, Hoyt!"

"Ready about!"

After nineteen tacks, the *New Zealand* still held on to her lead, but it was now no more than one boat length. The boats were closing on the finish line. The *Muskrat* was still closing, but was fast running out of time. The boats were on starboard tack. Before too long, they would be able to lay the committee boat on port.

As the *Muskrat* had worked her way up to the *New Zealand*, Hambden spoke up." We're getting ready to get trapped, Hoyt. We can barely clear the *New Zealand* if we tack. If we wait another minute, we'll have to wait for her to go." Hambden was right. They were three quarters of a boat length away and gaining very slightly. If they closed any more, they couldn't clear her stern to tack.

"Let's go now, Hoyt. We've got to go before the 'kiwis' can lay the committee.

"Hard alee!"

The *Muskrat* tacked over to port. The boys below had the jib trimmed in seconds.

The *New Zealand* tacked a little late. She was to weather of the *Muskrat* by two boat lengths, but the *Muskrat* was ahead of her by one and a half lengths.

Both boats were approaching the finish line nearly even. They had good speed on as they neared the end of the contest. It would be a photo finish. The *Muskrat* had fought her way back.

Sam was on his second bourbon and ordered his third. "What do you think, John?"

"I think I'm goin' to have another bourbon, Sam!"

Bradley was dying to know what was going on. It had been awhile since they had last tacked, and he wondered why. "How are we doin' up there, Hambden?"

Hambden had been eyeballing his hand-held compass. He was looking at the pin end. "I think we've got 'em, Bradley." Hoyt was concentrating on sailing the boat.

"Do you really think so, Hambden?" The crew was very excited.

Hambden replied, "They can't clear us if we tack, Hoyt, and we'll be on starboard. They'll either have to dip us and give us the lead or tack just as we do to stay out of our lee. If they dip, we'll tack back and cover. If they tack right away, we'll still be in the catbird seat. That is, if we go at the right time."

He leaned down and eyed the pin end through the compass built into the deck.

"Get ready, Hoyt. Not yet but very soon. This is the race. If we tack at the right time, I think we'll win. If we don't, we could give it away."

"Say when, Hambden! Be ready to tack gang, and for God's sake give me a good one."

"Let's go, Hoyt."

"Hard alee!" He threw the wheel over and the men below started rowing their guts out.

"Good trim!" Bailey yelled. Hambden looked below at the *New Zealand*.

"Get ready to tack back, boys!" He looked below him again and yelled at the top of his lungs.

"Starboard tack! Starboard!"

It was obvious the *New Zealand* couldn't clear the *Muskrat*. She was still on port tack and had no rights.

"She's tacking, Hoyt. Drive her, boy! We've got her where we want her now!"

Sky yelled aft, "We're not layin' the pin, Hambden."

Hambden took the glasses and got to weather in the cockpit. "Drive her, Hoyt. Go fast!" he said as he found the pin.

"We're fine! We're not layin' the mark, but only by a hair. That's right where I want to be. If we overstand, the *New Zealand* can sneak in there. We don't want that to happen. I don't want to be too close to that mark. Drive her, Hoyt! Drive her, boy! Be ready to tack, gang. One more good one and that should do it."

They were charging toward the pin and they were about ten

boat lengths from the line. The *New Zealand* was to leeward by
a boat length and a half. She was about a boat length ahead.
"They'll tack soon, boys! Be ready! No foul-ups! This is it!"
They now were less than six boat lengths from the mark and
they couldn't lay it. They were too far to leeward of it to shoot
up and make it. They would have to tack, but Hambden
wanted to wait for the *New Zealand*.
"There they go! Get ready!" Hambden watched the *New
Zealand* tack.
"Ready about!"
It was critical to tack at the right second and to have a
smooth one. As the *New Zealand* completed her tack and was
a boat length behind *Muskrat's* transom, Hambden gave the
order to go.
"Go, Hoyt! Trim! Trim!" The *Muskrat* tacked over to port
tack as the *New Zealand* slid beneath her, establishing an overlap. As the Muskrat settled down, the two twelves were
driving for the finish. Hoyt looked to leeward and just abeam
of his helm, he saw the bow of the New Zealand no more than
ten feet away.
"I'll watch the 'kiwis', Hoyt. You sail the boat." Hambden
wanted total concentration.
It was all over for the *New Zealand*. She had no room to tack
and she was in very disturbed air. She was just to leeward of
the *Muskrat*. She started losing a little speed as she pounded
into the seas off Freo. Everyone waited for the gun.
Hambden had called a brilliant race.
"Bang!" The finish gun fired. The entire crew went berserk.
Hoyt let out a "Ya-hoo!" Everyone held their fists in the air and
shouted for joy. The *Muskrat* had won her first race.
Hoyt put her into the wind and the jib dropped on deck.
Bradley and Drake popped up, each with a longneck. They

nearly killed each other, slapping the other on the back.

It took a few seconds for what had happened to really sink in. Hambden was thrilled beyond belief and felt very proud of the entire crew. He thought about that maneuver at the leeward mark and how well everyone had performed. "Nick, thank God you got here. Without you, we never could have done it today."

"Thanks, Hambden. It was quite a race."

As they passed the longnecks around, Hambden handed one to Hoyt.

"Here you go skipper! Nice race!" He looked at Hoyt and was taken aback. The skipper was in tears.

"Stop cryin', Hoyt. People will think we're sissies."

Hoyt chuckled and he held up his beer.

"You called some race, Hambden. I've never been more proud of a crew before. We did it, didn't we?"

It was a wonderful moment for the boys on *Muskrat*. It was a day that would not soon be forgotten.

Sam Johnson and John Dryden had gone through over half the bottle of bourbon. As they came alongside the *Muskrat* to give her a line, they saw that everyone had a Budweiser longneck.

"Where the hell did you get that beer?"

"That's what made the difference, Sam!"

"I'm not complaining, Bradley. Great race, boys!"

As they towed back to Fishing Boat Harbor, they overtook the *New Zealand* and passed her close by.

Bradley and Drake spotted Tanker leaning against the mast.

"There's the raccoon, Drake! Bet he had fun on that race."

Bradley raised his longneck and yelled to Tanker, "How ya feelin', bunky?"

Tanker never changed his expression. He just stared into

180

Bradley's eyes as the *Muskrat* went by. If looks could kill, Bradley would have been a dead man.

On the way in, Hoyt asked Nick if he knew what the problem was.

"I'm not sure, Hoyt, but I've got a hunch. I'll know for sure tomorrow."

That evening as they sat around their table at the P&O, the crew was anxious to find out what was happening back home. "Bring us up to date, Nick. What's going on in Oxford?"

"You are what's goin' on, Sam. You all are the main topic of conversation around town. Everybody wants to know what's goin' on down here. My phone never stops ringin'. You make the front page of the sports section 'bout every mornin'. You was on the front page of the 'Sunday Sun' last week. You're famous, boys."

"Is that really true, Nick? You mean a sailboat was on the front page of the 'Sun'?"

"You bet it was, Sky. They had a film on Channel 13 about you one night last week. I'm serious. The whole damn state is followin' you all. Wait 'til they hear about this race."

"That's all they talk about at your bar now, John. There's a great big sign over the bar. It says "Dryden's Bar & Grill, Future Home of the America's Cup."

Nick spent the rest of the evening telling the crew about what was happening back in Oxford. Everybody's family, friends, and girlfriends seemed to be fine. Those that were to come to Australia were very anxious according to Nick.

The fact that the *Muskrat* was getting a lot of publicity made them feel good, but they wished their following was in Australia with them and not halfway around the world.

Chapter Nine

The next day was an off day for the *Muskrat*. Nick hauled the boat and found the problem. The solution, he assured Sam and Hoyt, was simple and could be accomplished in just a few hours with the help of Spry and Covey, the close-mouthed Tilghman "Alanders." Because the problem involved the secret of *Muskrat's* phenomenal speed, Nick wanted no outside help.

On Friday morning, the *Muskrat* raced the *Italia*. The boat performed well and won easily. Nick was satisfied the boat was okay. She won her next three races, beating the *Courageous*, the *French Kiss* and the *USA* with Tom Blackaller at the helm. The *Muskrat* was on the move, winning five straight after their two defeats.

The *New Zealand* boat was doing very well since her defeat. The *Eagle* had a record of six wins, two defeats, and the *Stars and Stripes* had yet to be beaten. The *Muskrat* was scheduled to race the *Stars and Stripes* for the first time on November 5th.

The round robin was to continue until December 19th when the field would be cut to four boats. Every race was critical and the competition was fierce.

The arm wrestling competition had also been fierce. There were only four teams left. Twenty-eight had been beaten. Fortunately or unfortunately, Drake and Bradley were still in the running. Their next match was scheduled for November fourth. It was the same day as the running of the most popular horse race in Australia, the Melbourne Cup.

The P&O had been packed all day with fans waiting to see the running of the horse race. Betting and drinking were fast and furious. The race was scheduled for six o'clock, which was one hour after Drake and Bradley were to arm wrestle in the semi-finals.

At four o'clock, Bradley was frantically looking for Drake, who had not been seen since he wandered off from the compound at eleven that morning. After checking nearly every bar in Fremantle, Bradley finally found Drake at Keaten's Bar at four-thirty. He could barely talk.

"Gawd damn it, Drake! You can't even stand up and we got an arm wrestlin' match in a half hour!"

"Shee-it, I forgot!"

"You forgot! How the hell could you forget? We've got five thousand dollars on the line!"

"I'm sorry, Bradley. I'll do alright though. Let's go git 'em!"

Drake stood up and took one step toward the door. He tripped and fell, landing belly first over a chair and ending up under one of the tables in a pile. Everyone applauded as he got up.

"Gawd damn you, Drake, I could kill you. If we lose that five thousand dollars 'cause of you, I will kill ya, you son-of-a-bitch! Come on, let's go."

Drake stumbled out of the bar and headed for the P&O. Bradley held him by the arm, trying to keep him from falling.

They entered the bar on the dot of five and were greeted by their old bunky, Tanker. He and his partner had qualified for the wrestling finals earlier in the day.

"Well myte, looks like your partner's all ready to lose your money for you."

"If you don't want to lose your teeth, you'd better shut up, bunky!"

Tanker made a move toward Bradley, but was held back.

Drake was scheduled to wrestle first. The referee motioned him to the table. He could barely make his way through the huge crowd. As he stumbled to the wrestling table, Tanker was yelling at his opponent, "Don't you hurt my little bunky, myte!"

Bradley was very angry, but Drake was so stoned he didn't care.

The referee checked the grips and was about to blow the starting whistle when Drake went limp. His head dropped to the table and his body slowly found its way to the floor where he lay; passed out cold. Drake never made it to the match. Bradley's back was against the wall. He had to win twice to get into the finals. He won his first match without any problem and midway through the second, Tanker started on him.

"It's only five thousand dollars, bunky. Too bad your buddy passed out. You haven't got a chance now." He didn't let up.

Bradley was tiring. His opponent was very strong and had the advantage of only wrestling once. Both men's arms were still in the upright position. Bradley wasn't sure how much longer he could hold on.

The noise of the crowd and Tanker finally woke Drake. He got up and stumbled over to the table.

Bradley raised his head and saw Drake throw a right to Tanker's jaw. He knew he was in no condition to defend himself. Tanker would surely kill him. Bradley mustered every ounce of strength he had and pinned his man. He then went for Tanker. Tanker picked up a wooden chair and sent it flying across the room, just missing Drake. It found its way to the color television set, catching the twenty-five inch screen with one of its legs. The set broke into thousands of pieces as smoke poured out. The last picture seen on the tube was the gates opening and eleven thoroughbred horses starting the Melbourne Cup.

The place went berserk. Nearly everyone in the bar had wagered heavily on the race and had waited all day to see it. Half of the people ran out to find another bar and T.V. No one paid their tabs. The other half were so mad, they joined the fight.

Bradley overheard the bartender call the cops. He found Drake and they slipped out the front door. They got out in the nick of time. The cops arrived seconds later.

Drake and Bradley made their way back to the boat, barely eluding their fourth arrest. They felt badly about wrecking the P&O's bar, but felt good about getting to the finals.

At six-thirty, Sam Johnson arrived at the P&O to meet the crew for dinner. He couldn't believe what he saw. Chairs were strewn across the floor in bits and pieces. The television was still smoldering in the corner. Broken glass was everywhere. The place was a complete disaster. It looked as though a bomb had gone off.

"What the hell happened here, Jake?"

The bartender responded, "Mr. Johnson, the P&O has become the home away from home for you and the *Muskrat* crew. Everyone here at the hotel is happy about that except for one thing. If you don't hurry up and either win the cup or be eliminated, you're going to put a bar out of business that's been here for over fifty years. Drake and Bradley were involved in another fight. They started it all. Look at this place. I can't re-furnish this bar every couple of days."

"God damn those boys! I'm very sorry, Jake. Let me know what expenses you have incurred."

Jake's expenses were considerable. In addition to the physical damage, he had lost all of his business on one of the busiest nights of the year.

"Tell the crew to go ahead and order, Jake. I'd better get down to the jail. I'll bet the sheriff will want to keep'em for a while this time, and we go against the *Stars and Stripes* in the morning. God damn those two!"

"They didn't go to jail, Mr. Johnson. I saw them slip out right before the cops arrived."

"Thank God for that!"

When the rest of the crew arrived, they assured Sam that Bradley and Drake were safely aboard the *Queen* . After their meal, everyone headed back for a good night's sleep.

Sam thought to himself, "What the hell can I do with those boys? Every race is critical now. I've got to figure out something. It's too late to send them home. I don't have any replacements."

The race was to start at ten o'clock. The entire crew had been up since six-thirty looking for Bradley. It was now eight-thirty and he was nowhere to be found. Sam was beside himself.

"Well, that's it. Let's go. We'll have to race with three rowers today. God damn that Bradley."

This would be the first race against Dennis Conner and the *Stars and Stripes* . The records of the two boats were the best of all the challengers. The *Stars and Stripes* had yet to be beaten and the *Muskrat* had lost only four times. In addition to the initial two defeats, she raced twice in light to moderate air and lost both times. She seemed very slow in any air under fifteen. This could be a very serious problem in the later competition. The wind had a tendency to diminish as December approached and a significant drop in January and February was expected. The *Muskrat* was definitely designed for heavy weather.

Fortunately the winds were blowing a steady twenty knots, gusting to twenty-five. If the *Muskrat* could choose her weather, it wouldn't be any different than what the "Doctor" was providing today.

Back at Fishing Boat Harbor, Bradley Brown had finally been discovered.

"I say there, old bean, I believe you're on the wrong bucket!" One of the crew of the English twelve, *Crusader* had found Bradley curled up in the forepeak of their tender.

He had left Drake aboard the *Oxford Queen* while the rest of the crew was eating dinner. Bradley had found a pub and upon his return to the boat had gotten sidetracked. Somehow he had gotten into the English compound and passed out aboard their boat. Bradley slowly got up, and after some lengthy questioning from the English guards, headed for the *Oxford Queen*. The guards decided that he was still very intoxicated and even if he had seen anything, he wouldn't remember anyway.

Bradley stumbled around the harbor trying to locate the *Queen* and the *Muskrat*. He didn't realize they had left for the race. Finally, a policeman noticed him and wondered what he was up to. "What are you doing, old boy? You seem to be lost."

"Officer, you ain't gonna believe this, but I lost two things last night. One is fifty-five feet long and one is sixty-seven and I'll be damned if I can find either one of 'em!"

"I don't understand, sir."

"I'm lookin' for the twelve meter *Muskrat* and her tender the *Oxford Queen*."

"Oh, they're not here. The *Muskrat* is out racing *Stars and Stripes* at the moment."

"Oh shee-it! I'm in a heap of trouble. I've missed the gawd damn race. Sam's gonna kill me!"

At two fifteen, the *Muskrat* re-entered Fishing Boat Harbor.

The wind had held and to the joy of Sam, John and the crew, they had whipped Dennis Conner and the *Stars and Stripes* . They were the first to beat them.

Drake, Mark Litty and Herbert Loscomb were exhausted. It had been a very rough race, especially since Bradley had not been there to do his share of the rowing. He was not very popular with the rest of the crew.

Bradley was standing at the dock as the *Muskrat* was coming into the slip. "How'd you do, boys?"

Not a word was spoken. Bradley felt about an inch high. He knew he had really let everyone down. The *Queen* had tied up and Sam Johnson walked over to the *Muskrat* slip.

"You had a great race, Bradley. Where the hell have you been?"

"Oh, I'm sorry, Sam. Somehow I ended up sleeping on the wrong boat last night. You were gone by the time I could get here."

"You were the one that was gone, Bradley Brown. You were gone last night at the P&O. That little episode cost me five thousand dollars. What the hell is wrong with you? I can't believe you missed that race. You really disappointed everybody today. I don't know what the hell to do with you. I've seen hurricanes easier to control than you. I spend more time getting you and Drake out of trouble than I do with anything else. I'll spend more money keeping you two straight than I've got in the boat."

In spite of the crew problems, the *Muskrat* maintained an excellent record. She won eight out of her next ten races. The two times she lost was in light air. The *Stars and Stripes* beat her as did the *New Zealand* . Sam, Hoyt and the crew became very concerned about the diminishing breeze predicted for the next several weeks.

In the semi-finals, which started December 28, the *Stars and Stripes* beat the *New Zealand,* and the *Muskrat* beat *True North.*

Even though the air seemed to be getting lighter, the *Muskrat* and Dennis Conners were going head-to-head in the finals. There was one more boat to beat to become the challenger.

On the first day it was light and Conner won. The second and third day the Freo Doctor made his rounds, and the *Muskrat* took two straight. The fourth race was moderate to heavy, and even though Conner got an early lead, the boys from Oxford ended up winning. The final race was scheduled for January twenty-second and as luck would have it, the finals of the arm wrestling contest was to be held at ten o'clock the night before.

The girls from Oxford who were to arrive the twenty-second, the day of the race, came a day early. It seems that there had been so much excitement back home that Pucky at the travel agency had made arrangements to charter a plane just for the *Muskrat* followers from Oxford. Arrangements were made at the P&O for their stay.

Sam Johnson was petrified at the situation developing before him. There was one race that would determine the challenger, and the wives and girlfriends were to arrive the night before. To make matters worse, Drake and Bradley were to participate in the arm wrestling championship that night.

"Something has to be done," he thought to himself.

Sam Johnson called a meeting of the crew at ten a.m. the morning the girls were to arrive.

"Now listen to me, gang. Tomorrow is it. We'll either be picked as the challenger or be eliminated. Pray for heavy air. We've got to have a breeze.

"The girls arrive today at two thirty. I've arranged for those who want to go to drive to the airport and greet them. You will be driven to the Merlin where there will be a brief cocktail party and everyone will be my guests for an early dinner. Remember, the most important race of your lives is tomorrow at eleven o'clock. I know you're anxious to see the girls, but the race has to come first."

He looked Bradley and Drake in the eye. "If anybody gets into any trouble tonight, I'll never forgive them. Bradley, you and Drake are scheduled for an arm wrestling match tonight at ten o'clock. You will not make the match. Here is my personal check for five thousand dollars, which is what you would have won if you beat your opponents. After what I've spent to be in that race tomorrow, I can't afford you boys to be tired, even if it costs five thousand dollars. You are now officially out of the wrestling competition. Do you understand?"

Bradley and Drake looked at the rest of the crew and turned to Sam. "Yes sir," they both consented.

"To ensure that nothing goes wrong tonight, everyone is to meet me aboard the *Queen* at eight o'clock sharp. I will join you for the night. And I mean each and every one of you. Do you all understand?"

At two thirty, the entire crew met the charter and escorted them to the Merlin. It seemed nearly everyone who lived in Oxford was there. Even Mrs. Brinkley had made the trip. The wives and girlfriends were a welcome sight. It would be hard to say goodnight to them later, but everyone understood.

Their enthusiasm was incredible. Each and every one of the nearly two hundred and fifty people had been following the *Muskrat* through each and every race. Even though they were completely exhausted from their flight, they couldn't wait to get on their charter boat in the morning. The *Muskrat* just had to win, they thought to themselves.

To have this many people from Oxford fly halfway around the world meant everything to Sam, Nick, John Dryden and the crew. It was simply mind-boggling to think of what was taking place. After all the planning, building, traveling and racing, it had come down to the final race to be chosen the challenger. This time tomorrow they would be the challenger or it would all be over.

The party was a great success. Among the crowd who had made the trip was the tour director, Pucky Lappen. Sam got a kick out of hearing her story about getting old man Nick to Australia.

"You know Sam, Nick really didn't want to come down here. I sat him down and explained that the quickest flight would be by Buffalo to San Francisco and then to Honolulu and Perth. He said he wouldn't go. He was adamant. I impressed on him the fact that the race was in two days and this was the only way he'd make it. Well, we argued back and forth for a good fifteen minutes. Then Nick started pointing his finger at me and said, 'Pucky, I know what he wants me there for gawd damn it! I know all that, but let me tell you somethin', Missy. I'll go by bus, I'll take a train, I'll go by car or plane, but I ain't gittin' on no buffalo.'"

Sam nearly died, he was laughing so hard.

After a lovely dinner and many wonderful toasts, the *Muskrat* followers retired early.

Sam Johnson thought to himself, "I spent a fortune tonight, but it was worth it. If those people can travel to the other side of the world to support the *Muskrat*, the least I can do is buy them dinner. Besides, so far, I've kept my crew out of trouble."

During the evening's festivities, Drake and Bradley had remarked to each other that it was too bad they wouldn't have the chance to go head-to-head with Tanker.

"Shee-it, Drake, I'd like to lick that Tanker one time. Burns me up that we're just givin' him the prize money."

"Me too, Bradley. We never even found out who his partner was. Can't we sneak away just long enough to git that five thousand?"

"I know one thing, Drake. If we git caught by Sam or anybody in the crew we'll be like a pair a Canada geese with our wings set, pitchin' in front of a blind holdin' fourteen guns. We'll be dead!"

"We got to be real careful! That's for sure."

The crew wandered down to the *Queen*. Sam making sure no one was missing.

"Everybody aboard?" Sam asked, "Let's count heads."

Upon counting every crew member, he gave the order to untie the boat. "Let's get underway. We're anchoring out in the harbor tonight. Nobody's going to be tempted to go back for a nightcap." Bradley looked at Drake with disgust.

The *Oxford Queen* left her slip and headed out into the harbor where she dropped her hook for the night. Samuel E. Johnson, III was taking no chances.

At around nine fifteen, Bradley and Drake were feeling real badly that they were going to miss their shot at beating Tanker. The thought of forfeiting five thousand dollars was too much to take, especially to Tanker.

"How the hell can we git to that match, Bradley?"

"I'm thinkin', Drake. I'm thinkin'."

There was a long pause and then it hit him.

"I got it, Drake! I got it!"

"What, Bradley." How can we do it?"

"Drake, these blow-up mattresses we're sleepin' on will do the trick. They float. We can slip 'em overboard real quiet like and just lay on our bellies and paddle in with our arms. It'll work, Drake."

"But, Bradley! We'll git all wet!"

"Don't worry. What we're gonna do is steal a couple of them little plastic garbage bags so we can take dry clothes. We'll change when we git to shore."

"Good idea!"

Any plan that would mean a shot at Tanker sounded good to Drake. The two men packed their clothes in a garbage bag and crept over the side onto their makeshift rafts. It was overcast; the visibility was very poor.

"Where's the compass on this thing, Bradley?"

"Shut up and paddle, Drake!"

They arrived at the end of the jetty at nine forty five. Drake grabbed the garbage bag and headed for the beach further inland. There they changed into dry clothes and buried the wet ones in the sand. At exactly ten o'clock, Drake and Bradley arrived at the P&O Hotel Bar.

The place was packed as was expected. As they appeared at the door, the crowd gave them a thunderous ovation. Jake the bartender motioned them over.

"No trouble tonight, boys, understand?"

"Sure, Jake, no trouble."

They made their way through the crowd to the wrestling table. When they got there, Drake and Bradley couldn't believe their eyes. Standing before them was Tanker, and next to him his partner. It was none other than Blackdog. Bradley hadn't seen him since he knocked him out three months ago in Perth. Blackdog had a ferocious look on his face.

"I thought you yellow-bellies had chickened out!"

Drake kept his cool as Bradley spoke. "We ain't no yellow-bellies, Blackdog. You found that out in Perth. Let's git this wrestlin' match over with and then if you want to find out just how yellow we are, we'll meet you down at the Fishing Boat Harbor jetty. We ain't rippin' Jake's bar up no more."

The referee motioned Bradley to step up to the table. He looked Tanker in the eye as they jockeyed for the best grip, the whistle sounded and the contest was on. It took Bradley one minute twenty-two seconds to put Tanker down. The crowd went crazy. It was obvious they were rooting for the *Muskrat* team.

Tanker was furious. Fortunately, no one made any wise-cracks, for if they had, it would have been like setting off a bomb.

Blackdog was waiting for Drake as he stepped up. "I'm goin' to beat your American ass."

Drake didn't say a word. The whistle blew and in less than one second, Drake was pinned. Blackdog jumped up and down with his arms held high in the air. He had surprised Drake and timed the whistle perfectly. Drake never had a chance; the match was over before it ever started

Bradley took a deep breath. He knew the match was up to him. Drake felt like crawling in a hole. It wasn't a case of Blackdog necessarily being stronger, he just caught Drake off guard for a second, and that's all it took.

Bradley and Blackdog would wrestle for the tie breaker. The crowd was in a frenzy. Drake and Tanker stood next to each other as they watched their teammates jockey for the grip advantage.

The ref started the contest as the noise from the crowd grew.

Both men were super strong. Their arm muscles and veins bulged as they fought each other. Neither could budge the other's arm.

"Come on, Bradley! Git him!" Drake was cheering his partner on as Bradley's face turned a deep red.

They had been wrestling for nearly a minute and a half and he was feeling the effects of his first match. His arm didn't move an inch one way or the other, however.

Blackdog was obviously a powerful man. He didn't show the signs of strain like those on Bradley's face. It appeared that he was holding up better under the pressure of the match.

Bradley made two bursts of power, moving his opponent's arm about four inches toward a pin. Both times Blackdog held.

After nearly two and one half minutes, Bradley seemed to be weakening. Blackdog slowly moved his hand toward the table and a win. Drake looked on, wishing he could have a re-match. His partner was in trouble. It was almost over. Bradley's hand was six inches from the table.

"That's almost a thousand dollars an inch." Drake thought to himself. "Oh well. They still had the five Sam had given them."

The referee held his right hand up, ready to slam it on the table declaring Blackdog the victor.

Tanker was screaming, "Pin 'im, myte! Pin his American ass!"

Drake took exception, "Watch what you call my friend, bunky!"

"I'll call him anything I want to, Myte!"

"You'll be eatin a knuckle sandwich if you keep it up, bunk. I'll turn you every way but loose!"

Drake and Tanker were on each other.

Bradley thought to himself, "I can't give up. I can't let this jerk whip me; not after all I've been through to get here and to come away with nothin'! No way!"

He mustered some extra strength from somewhere and slowly brought his arm back to an upright position. The ref lowered his hand slowly. There would be no pin, not yet anyway. The crowd went crazy. Nearly everyone was cheering for Bradley.

I've got to find it within myself to pin this bastard. Bradley thought.

He moved Blackdog's arm about four inches, no more. Soon the arms were upright again. Bradley was in excruciating pain and nearly drained of strength. He made another move at Blackdog, giving it all he had. The arms moved about three inches, no more. The same thing happened and within seconds they were dead even.

Blackdog made a move and pulled his arm nearly eight inches toward a pin! Bradley looked as though he was about to give it up. He shut his eyes and dropped his head, hanging on for dear life.

He's wrestled his guts out no matter whether he wins or not, Drake thought to himself.

Bradley was going to give it one last shot. I've got one more burst left in me. I'll hold it as long as I can. If I don't do it now, I'm done. He pulled with all his might with his teeth clenched and eyes bulging. He brought Blackdog's arm through the upright position about four inches towards the pin. There the arms stopped, but Bradley kept giving it his all.

The crowd was hysterical. Drake was a mad man.

All of a sudden, above the noise of the crowd, was heard a loud "Click."

Everyone watched as Blackdog's right arm was pounded on the table. As Bradley slammed it down, a bone pushed through Blackdog's skin about a third of the way from his elbow and wrist. Bradley had broken Blackdog's arm and won the match. It was not a pretty sight. Blackdog was in tremendous pain. His arm lay on the table bleeding, as the bone stuck out through the skin.

The reaction from the crowd was mixed. Most were concerned for Blackdog, but many were hysterically cheering
Bradley's victory. The person making the most noise was
Drake. He slapped Tanker on the back. "How did you like that
one, bunky?"

Tanker turned and threw a right cross. Drake jumped on
him and they both ended up on the floor. Before another punch
was thrown, three cops were on top of them. Jake had wisely
called them before the match and they had been there the entire
time. It wasn't long before Drake and Tanker were in jail again.

Bradley had a beer and went down to the station. He
pleaded with the chief to let Drake go.

"We've got the most important race of our lives tomorrow.
Please officer. I'll do anything to get my buddy out of jail. Mr.
Johnson is anchored out on a boat for the night and can't be
reached." Bradley was damned glad of that. If Sam knew what
was going on, he would kill both of them.

"Do you know how many times you and your friend have
been here? Your buddy spends more time here than he does on
your damned boat. I should have locked him up and thrown
away the key months ago. You boys are bad actors."

"But officer, please! Just give us one more chance. Please!
We race tomorrow to see who will challenge you for the
America's Cup. Please officer. I beg you."

The chief of police sat thinking for a few seconds.

"I'll tell you what I'll do. You pay Drake's fine and I'll
release him."

"Great! No problem, Chief. How much?"

"Ten thousand dollars."

"Ten thousand dollars! Gawd damn, chief! Are you shittin'
me?"

"Mister, you want your buddy out? That's it! Ten thousand

smackers, right now."

Bradley couldn't believe it. It would mean giving up the five that Sam had given them plus the five that he had worked so hard for in the tournament. He then thought of the alternative and quickly decided to pay up. The cop had him where he wanted, and there was nothing Bradley could do. He and Drake wandered back to the P&O. Bradley was so mad, he couldn't see straight. He wasn't sure who he was mad at the most, the Chief or Drake.

"Gawd damn you, Drake! You git drunk and pass out at matches, you lose tonight and I still win us the five thousand dollars and what the hell do you do? You git thrown in the slammer and we lose everything. You really piss me off, Drake!"

"I'm sorry, Bradley. Tanker started it."

"Well, let's have a beer and drown our sorrows."

The boys sat down among the crowd at the P&O. Everyone wanted to buy Bradley a beer. He became a real celebrity by winning two matches and breaking Blackdog's arm to win the championship. He soon forgot about the ten thousand dollars; after all, they were the champions.

It was almost two a.m. when the boys got back to the jetty. They were not in real great shape and couldn't find where they had buried their clothes.

They stumbled down to the end of the jetty and got on their mattresses. Visibility was very poor. It was completely overcast and they could hear thunder in the distance.

"We'd better get going, Drake, before a squall hits."

They headed away from the jetty paddling on their stomachs. After going about ten yards, Bradley noticed Drake wasn't keeping up. "Come on, Drake, paddle!"

Drake didn't move, so Bradley went back. He found him

passed out on the raft.

"Gawd damn it, Drake! Wake up." He slapped him on the head and Drake came to.

"Don't go to sleep on me boy, it's gonna squall in a minute. We gotta git to the *Queen* . Come on!"

Bradley headed out again. A breeze was picking up out of the northwest, pushing them toward the entrance of the harbor.

"Hurry up, Drake. We ain't got much time."

Just then, there was a loud clap of thunder right on top of them.

"Paddle like hell, Drake! Drake!"

Bradley couldn't find him in the total darkness. He was almost to the *Queen* as the wind began to really kick up.

"Where the hell is Drake?" he said to himself.

He yelled his name as loud as he could, but heard nothing in response. The wind was blowing hard and the rain had just started as Bradley got to the *Oxford Queen* . He held himself up, holding on to the rail as he stood on the rubber mattress. He still couldn't see Drake. The rain made visibility near zero as it came down harder and harder. The wind was gusting to near forty.

"Drake could be in real danger. Why in the hell did we ever go ashore?" he said to himself.

Just as a bolt of lightning lit up the harbor, Bradley spotted Drake. He appeared to be passed out on his raft and was at the entrance of Fishing Boat Harbor. Drake and his raft were being blown out into the ocean.

Bradley didn't know what to do. If he woke up the crew Sam would find out what was going on, but on the other hand, he couldn't let his buddy drift out in the ocean, passed out on a rubber raft. He climbed aboard and woke up Hoyt.

"Drake's in trouble, Hoyt!"

"What kind of trouble?"

"It's stormin' out, and he's passed out on a raft in the ocean."

"You're drunk, Bradley. Go back to sleep."

"I may be drunk, Hoyt, but Drake's in trouble. He's passed out in the ocean on a gawd damn mattress. We've got to go git him."

"Bradley, I know this is a dumb question, but how did Drake pass out on a mattress and end up in the Indian Ocean?"

"He passed out cause he drank too much, and he's in the ocean cause the wind is northwest, Hoyt."

"Gawd damn you and Drake! We got a race in a few hours and we've already got one of our crew on the course and on a gawd damn mattress to boot!"

"Come on, Hoyt. We gotta git him quick."

The deafening sound of the *QE II's* horn woke Drake up. She was making her landfall at Fremantle and was about a half mile from the mouth of the Swan River. She, along with several other ships, had come to see the cup races scheduled to start in a week. Along with the *QE II*, the *Achillo Lauro* and the *Viking III* were also to arrive within the next several days.

The storm had subsided, but the seas were still very high. As Drake's mattress crested at the top of a roller, he looked up and spotted the bow of *QE II*.

"What the shit is that?" he said out loud. "Gawd damn! Its a ship! Shee-it! I'm done for."

Hoyt fired up the engine on the *Oxford Queen* as Bradley went forward to handle the anchor. The rain had stopped and the wind had subsided. Glenn and Pete came into the wheel house.

"What's goin' on, Hoyt?"

"You ain't gonna believe it, boys, but be careful if Sam gets up. We can't let him know what's really goin' on. Drake's passed out on a mattress in the ocean."

"What? No way!" Glenn, of course, didn't believe the story. They got underway and headed out of Fishing Boat Harbor. Suddenly Samuel E. Johnson, III appeared. "What the hell are you doing, boys?"

Bradley answered, "We just drug our anchor during the storm, Sam. No problem. Go back to bed."

Everyone took a deep breath.

"Okay, boys. Sure I can't help?"

All four people in the wheel house quickly assured Sam that everything was under control and his assistance was not necessary.

As they entered the ocean, Hoyt saw the *QE II*.

"Jesus Christ! There's a ship comin' in! I hope it doesn't run over Drake!" He throttled up and turned on the spot light.

"Bradley, take this light and see if you can find him."

The horn of the ship sounded again as it got closer to the raft. Drake was paddling for all he was worth, trying to get out of the ship's path. He would periodically check the ship's range lights and paddle at a right angle. It seemed as though he would make it.

"I've got him, Hoyt. He's just to starboard of the ship. Follow the beam of light."

The *QE II* passed safely by and entered the Swan. Hoyt and the crew hauled Drake aboard and returned to Fishing Boat Harbor. Drake had barely survived the ordeal. It had been another memorable night, winning the arm wrestling championship, another trip to jail, losing ten grand, and nearly being run over by the *QE II*. It had been a long night, especially for the two wrestlers.

The race was scheduled for eleven o'clock and Sam had the crew up at six thirty. They would put the *Queen* in her slip and grab breakfast at the P&O.

"Except for dragging anchor in the squall, did everyone get a good night's sleep?"

"Sure did, Sam."

"Bet you're glad you and Drake stayed away from the wrestling last night, eh Bradley?"

"Sure thing, Sam."

"By the way, you boys want me to keep that five thousand for you 'til we get back home? Knowing you two, you might lose it."

Drake and Bradley looked each other in the eye. "No thanks, Sam. That ain't necessary."

As they wandered up the street to the P&O, they noticed people everywhere. "You know where these people came from Drake? I heard it on the radio this morning. The *QE II* came in during the night. She's pretty big. Have you ever seen her, Drake?"

I seen her once, Sam. She's big all right. Drake thought to himself, If Sam only knew how big she can look.

There were several ships already in Fremantle and a total of fourteen cruise ships would arrive for the final cup races. Freo was bustling. The America's Cup had swept the town off its feet. No matter who you talked to, the topic of conversation involved the twelves and who would be in the races beginning January thirty-first. In every window there was an America's Cup display. You couldn't turn on a radio or television without hearing about the races.

As the crew entered the P&O, they received a loud applause. The place was full of the people from Oxford, including many of the wives and girlfriends. Drake went over to his girlfriend Harriet and gave her a big hug and kiss.

"How did you sleep, Harriet?"

"Believe it or not, I didn't sleep very well. My room is just above the bar and there was quite a commotion down here last night. Did you get a good night's sleep? You've got a big race today!"

"Not really."

Among the rest of the group was Mark's wife Sue and Hambden's girlfriend Beau. It was great to see the girls, but it was now time to concentrate on the race.

On the tow out to the starting line, it looked like a cattle herd. There were more than two thousand spectator boats of all shapes and sizes.

With the exception of the girlfriends and wives who were on the *Queen* , the rest of the Oxford group went out on an eighty foot sightseeing boat called the *Vista III*.

The sailing conditions were a mixed bag. The wind was a little on the light side at twelve to fifteen. This concerned the *Muskrat* boys very much. On the other hand, as a result of the storm, the seas were large. This, they thought, would be to their advantage.

At ten-thirty, the *Muskrat* separated from her tender. It was time to decide whether or not they would race for the America's Cup.

Chapter Ten

Hambden decided to go to the light number one and stow the number two to starboard and the heavy number one to port. "Let's fire up the jib, boys. These seas are huge today. Let's get goin' and she'll settle down."

Nick and Sam were listening to the weather forecast back on the *Queen* . "Sam, I sure hope the Doctor makes his rounds today. It's too light for us right now."

"This race will be determined by the Doctor, Nick. I hope he comes. He's got to come today. He's just got to."

They started the race in twelve knots; much too light for the *Muskrat* .

There was no clear winner at the start. Conner was the weather boat, but the *Muskrat* had clear air and hit the line right at the gun.

As the two boats worked their way to the weather mark, the *Stars and Stripes* appeared to be moving slightly faster. She was hobby-horsing quite a bit, but she was still out footing the *Muskrat* . As they rounded the mark, she had a twelve second lead. On the next leg, she lengthened her lead, but only by six seconds. The crew of the *Muskrat* was very concerned, but they knew the race was far from over.

"I wish the air would pick up, Hoyt. Just hang in there best you can and pray." Hambden wished for more breeze.

On the next weather leg, the wind got lighter. Sam and the

crowd on the *Queen* were beside themselves. The *Muskrat* was slowing down. It was even too light to gain any ground when they tacked. Things looked very grim.

"She's slow as shit, Hambden!"

"Just do the best you can, Hoyt. Ease the jib three inches, Bailey. Come on, Doctor, it's time to make a call."

It was nerve-wracking. There they were in the middle of the final race with no air. Thousands of spectators were watching their performance. The Oxford contingency was there for their first race. Film crews were everywhere, including three in choppers. They prayed the air would fill.

"Hang in there, Hoyt. We've got five legs to go. There is a lot of race yet."

Dennis Conner beat the *Muskrat* to the mark by twenty three seconds. The spinnaker set was perfect on both boats. All of the sail handling had been flawless.

"Wind's up, Hoyt! It's pickin' up fast, boy! Drive this gawd damn bucket!"

The wind was coming in. The Doctor seemed to be on his way.

Old man Nick was in front of the wheel house pointing toward something, "Look Sam. See that air comin' in? It'll be here in a second. Thank God. Maybe we can git back in this race."

"Why the hell did it take so long, Nick? It may be too late. The *Muskrat* caught the breeze first and made up a lot of ground on Conners. "We're eatin' her up, boys. Let's have a good jibe." They rounded the reaching mark only twelve seconds behind the *Stars and Stripes* and were closing the gap. The wind continued to build and as they approached the leeward mark, they established an overlap on Conners.

The wind was gusting to twenty-two and seemed to be

building.

"Number two, boys. Quick! Change to the number two."

Schuyler quickly popped the starboard locker open and attached the halyard as Vaughn changed the sheets.

"When it settles down, number three in the locker. Let's go. Fire her up!"

It took just a couple of seconds for the change and when they were three boat lengths from the mark, Hambden yelled to Conner, "Room at the mark. We've got an overlap."

Conner responded, "You'll have it, skipper, but not an inch more than you need." Conner felt a little trapped. He knew he should have his number two up, but there was no time. They rounded with the number one and then sent two men forward to change. To say that Conner and his crew were envious of the *Muskrat's* system was an understatement. By the time the sail change was made, the *Muskrat* had taken the lead.

The *Oxford Queen* was within fifty yards of the leeward mark as they rounded. She had a special pass which enabled her to follow the race more closely than the others; a small token to the owners of the twelves who had put up the millions of dollars. The Oxford gang was going crazy. The crew aboard the *Muskrat* had no trouble hearing them as they rounded.

The boats thrashed toward the weather mark. Conner tacked every minute or so, but every time he did, he lost a few feet to the *'Rat* .

They were on the sixth leg of the race with only two to go; a run and then a beat back to the finish. The winds were building, gusting to nearly thirty. Hoyt had the boat moving well. The crew had performed flawlessly. They were all business on this day. The *'Rat* was on the move.

"Heavy chute, boys! Gawd damn, make it a good one! This is your last set to become the challenger!" Hambden was excited. "Only two laps, gang!"

One mistake now and it could mean the ball game. They all knew the master was right on their tail. If anyone could outguess Hambden and his crew, it would be Dennis Conner. They were well aware that he was the best. The *Muskrat* pulled around the weather mark only nine seconds ahead.

"Chute up! Let's go! Jib down!"

The spinnaker went up in a flash. It filled with a tremendous loud pop. It was pulling beautifully. Vaughn Downes was standing forward of the port shrouds, unaware that he was outboard of the spinnaker sheet. When it filled, the sheet snapped tight and threw Vaughn overboard.

"Vaughn's over, Hoyt! Shit!" Sky yelled aft.

"Gawd damn it! That's the race! I can't believe it! Might as well git the chute down, Hambden!" Hoyt was stunned.

"Is that someone overboard?" Nick asked Sam.

"Where?"

"Look's like the *Muskrat* may have lost somebody. Oh no!"

It was a heart-sinking moment for everyone who backed the *Muskrat*. To come this far and have it end on the next to the last leg was too much to bear. After all the planning, all the money, all the sailing; after an entire town came halfway around the world; to lose like this was just too much. Hoyt got ready to turn around and go back to pick up Vaughn.

"Trip the chute, Sky!"

"Bullshit, Hoyt! Don't touch that chute. Drive this son of a bitch!" Hambden gave orders to continue.

"But, Hambden, Vaughn's over. We got to go back for him. We'll be thrown out."

"Thrown out! Shee-it! If we go back now, it's all over. I ain't givin' up yet, not with this lead. Sail this gawd damn boat."

"What about Vaughn? Do we just leave him to the sharks?"

"Just sail this boat, Hoyt. Boys, you got to forget about Vaughn for awhile. Concentrate on this boat and listen to me. There's over two thousand boats out here. Vaughn ain't gonna drown. The rule says we gotta finish the race with the crew we started with, but it don't say nothin' more. I got a good loran fix on Vaughn when he went over. We'll try to git him on the next leg. I know one thing, if we go back now the *Muskrat* has lost for sure. We gotta go on boys. It's a long shot, but we just gotta. Besides, I don't think a shark can git hungry enough to eat Vaughn. Did you smell him when he got aboard this mornin'?"

The *Muskrat* continued on and seemed to widen her lead on the downwind leg.

Vaughn Downes felt like drowning himself, he was so disgusted. He couldn't figure why the boat had continued, however. It was a very unusual position to be in to see the two twelves sail away and be left in the middle of a race course surrounded by thousands of boats.

The spectators were all dumbfounded. The helicopters zoomed down, one coming within a few yards of Vaughn, filming the *Muskrat* crew member adrift in the Indian Ocean.

The *Muskrat* jibed and headed for the mark. The wind had steadily increased and was now gusting over thirty.

"Number three jib!" Hambden was considering reefing the main.

They rounded the mark twenty-three seconds ahead.

To find Vaughn, get him aboard, and not lose their lead would take a miracle. Still, Hambden thought they had a shot!

"If we see him, we've got to get him in on the leeward side. Everybody get to leeward with a line that has a loop in it. He should be able to grab one of them as we go by. We'll luff the sails for a second, but that's all. We can't let Conner git by us.

I want everybody to go to the leeward side at the last second. I'll tell you when. Conner is sharp and if he sees the commotion, he'll pick that time to tack so we can't cover. Now, I'll make up the lines for you and coil them up, right here. Does everybody know what to do?" They seemed to understand.

The *Muskrat* was widening her lead. This was her weather. It was a downright shame that Vaughn had gone overboard. She would win without a doubt had he stayed on board.

"We're gettin' close to where he went over. Everybody keep a sharp eye out."

Nobody saw anything. It would be very difficult to spot him in the rough seas.

"Anybody see anything?"

"'Fraid not, Hambden."

"We're gettin' fairly close to the finish line. He's got to be right around here somewhere. God damn it! I can't believe this is happening!"

They were on port tack covering Conner and the *Stars and Stripes*. The finish line was less than a quarter mile ahead. Time was running out. It looked like it was all over.

"I guess somebody has picked him up, boys."

"I'm afraid you're right, Hoyt."

It was the lowest the crew had felt in their lives. There they were in the middle of two thousand boats sailing under a blimp, planes, and choppers, and they felt lost. They were winning the race to be the challenger, but they would surely watch the *Stars and Stripes* go to the line against *Australia* . It was an all-time low for everyone.

Suddenly, Hambden heard someone on the foredeck, "There he is, Hambden! There's Vaughn. See him?" Jimmy Firth was pointing to weather.

"I don't see him, Jim."

"He's dead to weather, right dead to weather."

"I still don't see him. Should we tack?"

"Not yet, Hambden. Don't you see him?"

"No! Where is he in relation to the mark?"

"He's standin' on it, Hambden."

"He's what?"

"He's standin' on the mark!"

"I don't believe it! Vaughn's a genius!"

"There goes Conner, Hambden! He's tacked, let's cover."

"Let him go. We've got to sail our own race now. Listen to me. We've got about a twenty second lead. If we do this just right, it may be enough. I've got a plan. Listen up." The entire crew gained new life as if they had been charged by a bolt of lightning. They were intent on Hambden's plan.

"When we can lay the mark, we'll go over to starboard tack. Now, by Vaughn being on the pin end of the finish line, that's the same as the boat hitting the mark. We'll go to the mark on starboard.

"We'll go right up to it, and Vaughn will jump aboard. By doing that, we'll have our crew and will have crossed the finish line. They won't fire a gun 'cause we've hit the mark. We have to re-round. We'll tack, jibe and go through the line again. You'll have to trim like hell after the jibe, understand? It's going to be tricky and Conner is on our tail."

They continued on port until Hambden felt he could lay the finish line and tacked. The *Stars and Stripes* had gone to the left side of the course, gambling they would get a break in a wind shift.

As they got closer to the bouy, Hambden looked at the mark with his binoculars. "I can't believe it! I can't believe it!"

"What, Hambden? What do you see?"

"Vaughn's naked. He ain't got no clothes on."

Vaughn Downes had peeled his clothes off so he could swim to the bouy. As he was getting his pants off, his shorts came off too. There he was, standing on the pin end of the finish line, naked as a jaybird, waving his hands in the air so the *Muskrat* would spot him. Around him were over two thousand spectator boats loaded with people hysterically laughing at this poor soul standing on the bouy without a stitch of clothes. Three helicopters were swooping down on Vaughn with their camera crews filming away. The race was being telecast live throughout the world.

On the other end of the line was the race committee. They were very confused and were not at all sure what was going on. Back on the *Oxford Queen*, Sam was confused as anyone. His boat was approaching the line in first place, heading for the pin on which stood a naked crewman.

"We see you, Vaughn! Jump aboard as we come by!" Hambden yelled.

Conner had tacked back to port, and was going for the finish. He would hit the committee boat end of the line.

"Conner has caught us! This move at the finish has to be perfect gang. Hoyt! Roll that wheel hard, boy. It's gonna be inches!"

The *Muskrat* came within a foot of the mark. Vaughn jumped aboard as the big twelve tacked. The boat headed downwind, and Allison eased the huge mainsail.

"Big trim, boys!" She trimmed the main and jibed. After another ease, she called for trim again.

Hambden looked down at the committee boat end of the line. Conner was almost there with a full head of steam on.

"Luff her up, Hoyt!" He shot her into the wind as Conner was just about to cover up the race committee flag.

"Bang!"

211

The gun fired—the *Muskrat* won.

The jubilation aboard the *Muskrat* was like a freshly opened champagne bottle overflowing. The sounds of celebration spewed from everywhere. Horns blew from nearly every boat ranging in size from huge sightseeing vessels to tiny fifteen foot runabouts. The people lining the shore went crazy as the helicopters buzzed around the Goodyear blimp. People around the world who had watched the live TV coverage had never seen a more exciting conclusion to a sporting event. They certainly had never witnessed a more unusual one.

Sam Johnson and Nick Benson shook hands. "We did it Sam! We did it!"

"I can't believe it, Nick! I just can't believe we won."

"Great race, Hoyt!"

"You won that one, Hambden."

"No. We all won it. Gawd damn, I can't believe we've done it! The *Muskrat* is actually going to sail for the America's Cup!"

"Watch out, Hambden!" Bradley and Drake came rushing on deck.

"What's wrong boys?"

Hambden soon understood as Bradley and Drake headed for the leeward rail and got sick.

"You ever seen the *QE II* , Drake?"

"Go to hell, Hambden!"

Soon Drake and Bradley joined in the celebration, as did Vaughn Downes. Vaughn was quite a sight as he stood in the number two sail bag with the draw strings tightened around his waist.

"What happened to your skivvies, Vaughn?" Schuyler asked.

"They came off with my pants."

"Cap'n, you was a pretty sight standin' on that buoy. You

realize how many people seen you? You was on television clean around the world, boy."

Drake piped in, "Shee-it, Vaughn, if you was, you'll have to go to Mars to git a date. You're in a heap a trouble."

The crew broke up laughing.

"Go to hell, Drake!"

Upon lowering her sails, the *Muskrat* hooked up to the *Oxford Queen* and started towing in. The gang on the tender were yelling and screaming as the spectator fleet surrounded them.

Dennis Conner and the crew of the *Stars and Stripes* came by. "Well done, boys. Great race!" The crew responded with a wave. Conner and his crew were a class act indeed.

As they entered the harbor, two fire boats had positioned themselves on either side of the breakwater. They threw two huge columns of water forming an arch through which the *Queen* and the *Muskrat* passed. The horns had never stopped since the finish, and they stepped up their sounds as the *Muskrat* re-entered the harbor.

It was an incredibly moving experience for the *Muskrat* crew and a thrill for the gang aboard the *Queen* .

"What's wrong, Hoyt?" Hambden looked aft and saw his skipper in tears again.

"Come on, Hoyt. Twelve meter skippers ain't supposed to cry." Hoyt fought back the tears and wiped his eyes.

"I can't believe this, Hambden. I just can't believe it." He started bawling.

"Shee-it, Hoyt. What are you cryin' 'bout?" Drake was feeling a little better, "You wasn't on the buoy naked with all them people laughin' at ya, Vaughn was. He's the one ought to be cryin'."

What a celebration they had ashore. Each and every crew

member was an instant celebrity, especially Vaughn Downes. Fremantle was like a bee hive, buzzing as a result of the race. Newspaper and magazine reporters were standing in line to get an interview with one of the crew. Television crews lined up outside the compound fence.

The crew joined the girls aboard the *Queen* for a private celebration. The *Vista III* motored into Fishing Boat Harbor and made a pass close by the *Oxford Queen*. Everyone aboard gave them a loud ovation as the *Vista* sounded her horn. She then headed out and up the Swan River.

Drake was the first to leave for the P&O. He wanted to see Jake and warn him that Sam and the girls were unaware of last night's festivities. As he left the compound, the press attacked.

"Was that race the most exciting thing you've ever experienced, Drake?"

"Shee-it, no! Not by a mile."

"What could ever top it?"

"Oh, I had an experience with a lady last night that was a lot more exciting."

Everyone laughed. "She must have been quite a lady, Drake!"

"Yea, she was a queen!"

"Seriously, that was some race. Tell us about it."

"Well, we put our sails up at the ten minute gun and I went below to handle the winches. We started the race and when the finishing gun fired, I came back up. There was a lot of boats around at the start and finish, but you'll have to ask somebody else what they seen durin' the race. All I seen was Bradley, and I know you don't want his picture in the paper. Shee-it! You'd lose every customer you got. It'd be like bein' just south of a north bound mule; not very pretty."

The interview continued and by the time Drake had gotten

to the P&O, Sam and some of the crew had already arrived.
When he walked in, he noticed something new hanging on the
wall over the arm wrestling machine:

1987 Arm Wrestling Champions
Bradley Brown & Drake Cochran

Shee-it, Sam knows. I'm in a heap of trouble, Drake thought
to himself. He noticed that Bradley was already there, so he
made a beeline for him.

"Has Sam seen the sign?"

"I'm sure he has, Drake, but he ain't said nothin' about it
yet."

"Thank Christ we won today. At least he's in a real good
mood."

"I'd better tell Harriett what happened. "

When everyone had arrived, Jake the bartender came over
to the table carrying a large tray on his shoulder.

"Boys and girls, I have a little surprise for the 1987 challenger for the America's Cup."

He lowered the tray onto the table and revealed a case of
Budweiser longnecks. Everyone applauded.

"I have made arrangements to have your brand in stock as
long as you are here. Congratulations!" It was a wonderful
surprise.

"Now this is officially the headquarters of the *Muskrat* !"
Hoyt exclaimed as he held his longneck up.

"To the *Muskrat*, the official challenger for the America's
Cup!" another crewmember toasted. The party lasted well into
the night. Not a word was mentioned by Sam about the sign on
the wall, he felt he could deal with that later. Tonight was a
night to celebrate.

Drake told Harriett that he had participated in the finals but
upon winning went straight to the boat. He made no mention

of his trip into the ocean. Luckily, she didn't ask about the money.

The crew slowly gathered at the P&O the next morning, most were well hungover. The morning newspaper was a very popular item during the races. Usually there were several interviews with the crew of yesterday's race and all the latest news connected with every facet of the cup. This morning's issue was of particular interest.

On the front page was a picture of Vaughn Downes standing on the finishing buoy, waving his arms to the *Muskrat*, which could be seen beating to weather in the background.

The caption under the picture read, *"Muskrat Crew Barely Wins."* Everyone got a kick out of it, including Vaughn. He knew he couldn't beat them, so he'd better join in their fun. Within the first ten minutes he was in the hotel, he had signed twenty of the papers.

As Drake wandered in, he was met by his girlfriend, Harriet. "Damn you, Drake Cochran! What the hell do you think you're doin' down here?"

"I'm racin' sailboats!"

"You'll be racin' your ass home, if you aren't careful. Sit down here." Harriet was as mad as a hornet and Drake didn't know why.

"Read that! What have you been doing down here? Damn you, Drake!"

Drake read the part she had pointed out.

"Drake Cochran said the excitement of the race didn't compare to the encounter he had the night before with a newfound lady friend. The girls of Freo should be proud to have such a compliment paid by our American sailor. He called her a "Queen."

Drake knew he had some explaining to do. "Now Harriett,

this ain't exactly what it sounds like. She weren't really a lady and she weren't a queen like you think either."

"Damn you, Drake! That's worse! You mean you been messin' around with some slut down here?"

"No, Harriet. She was a boat."

"A boat! You mean she was a fat slut! I'm gonna knock the shit outta you, Drake!"

"Harriet, you don't understand. I was asleep on my bed and this big boat was comin' at me."

"Drake, where did she come from? You was anchored in the middle of the harbor. Did she swim out to your boat?"

"No, Harriet. Gawd damn it. I was in my bed in the ocean and the queen was comin' toward me. "

"Now you're in bed in the ocean, and she's a queen again. I give up!"

It took awhile, but Drake finally explained to Harriet what had really happened.

"Oh, honey, I'm sorry. Thank God you're all right." Then she got mad all over again. "You mean to tell me you and Bradley lost ten thousand dollars?" It took some time, but she finally settled down.

Sam Johnson and Nick Benson arrived. Sam noticed that *Australia III* had beaten *Kookaburra* three days before and there were only two days left in the finals to determine the defender. January fifteenth would be the last day of competition.

Nick worried about his design in light air. He knew that in February, the winds tended to go light. It had almost happened the day before against the *Stars and Stripes* . He gave some thought to making some changes in the boat over the next week.

The first race was scheduled for January 31st and it was only the twenty-fourth. A lot could be done in a week, and all the tools and facilities in the world were at his disposal. After yesterday's victory, a representative from every American syndicate offered all of their manpower, expertise, sails and gear. They all wanted the cup back in the U.S. just as badly as the *Muskrat* crew.

Nick and Sam discussed all of the possibilities. They decided to meet with a representative of each U.S. syndicate over lunch and then make a decision. The phone calls were made, and a meeting called for twelve thirty at the *Muskrat* compound.

The *Muskrat* was moved into the shed so the experts could see what she looked like underneath. They all arrived by one o'clock. All six syndicates sent their representatives: The *U.S.A.*, *Courageous*, *America II*, *Heart of America*, *Eagle* and the *Stars and Stripes*. Each representative was amazed at the secret. It was so simple, yet such a breakthrough.

Olin Stepens asked old man Nick, "How in the world did you figure this out?"

"My grandaddy figured out the secret, and I just developed it. She's a little different, ain't she?"

"I'll say she's different. I've been designing twelves for a good many years and I've got to hand it to you, Nick."

The meeting lasted an hour and a half and a decision was made. There would be no changes to the *Muskrat*. They agreed that the secret should not be altered. She had beaten every other challenger and now was not the time to alter her lines. It would be a gamble not to change her, since the air could easily go light, but they felt to change her now would be a bigger gamble.

Another decision was made; everyone felt it was critical to keep the Aussies guessing. It was decided to pretend they were going to make major changes. A plan was made to convince the world that the *Muskrat* was being altered. There was to be a large "work force" that would enter and leave the boat shed around the clock.

A new crew would arrive at conspicuous times. One would enter the compound at nine thirty in the morning and leave at five thirty when another crew would relieve them. Another shift would go to work during the night. This would convince everyone that the boat was being completely rebuilt. Sam assured them that there would be plenty of beer and beds inside the shed, in addition to movies to help keep them busy. The object of the scheme was to convince the Aussies that the *Muskrat* was undergoing a radical change even though the *Muskrat* syndicate was going to rely on their secret and leave the boat as it was.

After the final race on January twenty-fourth, it was the *Australia III* that became the defender. It was finally decided after four full months of racing, that the *Muskrat* would go against the *Australia III* for the America's Cup.

Immediately following the final race, the *Australia III* was hurriedly moved into her shed and a crew of twenty-three people entered the compound. It appeared as though she would undergo a major facelift, and the number of guards on duty at her compound was doubled.

Speculation was rampant around Freo. Everyone wondered what the boats would be like after the changes were made. Little did they know that the Muskrat would enter the America's Cup race January thirty-first exactly like she was on her last race.

The *Australia III* had also been designed for heavy air. That is why she had gained her victory in the finals. However, it seemed obvious that her syndicate felt modification was in order, to what extent no one knew. They wouldn't find out until January thirty-first when at one o'clock the starting gun would fire.

On the morning of the twenty-fifth, the newspapers reported little else other than the news of the cup races. The event dominated everything. The headlines read,*Two New Boats To Race For The Cup.*

The article explained that both the *Australia III* and *Muskrat* were undergoing major surgery preparing for the lighter airs predicted for February. It detailed the elaborate security that surrounded each boat, describing every precaution that had been taken. Sam felt the article had given too much information on the security measures.

Nick tried to find if there was a reliable long range weather forecast, but quickly concluded that there wasn't. He'd just have to wait and see what mother nature had in store for them.

The crew was enjoying these days off with the girls and their friends from Oxford and the Eastern Shore. The fact that so many had come meant the world to them. It had been a very long and sometimes lonely four months. They were having a wonderful time showing everyone Freo and Perth.

Drake had great fun explaining how you caught some of the local game, including kangaroos and particularly the duck-billed platypus.

Meanwhile, the crews doing the work on the *Muskrat* were showing up faithfully. So far, no one from the outside had figured out that there really was no work taking place.

On the night of the twenty-fifth, there was a big party planned by the Eastern Shore contingency. It was to be given by the Marylanders to show the *Muskrat* how grateful they were for the tremendous effort put forth.

In order that everyone could attend, when the work crews relieved each other at five thirty, they played a little trick. Thirteen people showed up in a large van which was driven inside the compound. They got out of the van and went inside the shed. Each one walked over to a pile of clothes already there and changed shirts, some adding a hat. Then the same thirteen turned right around and got back in the van leaving a tape recorder playing the sounds of the day before. It was off to the Merlin for a night of celebration.

The party was a huge success, especially the dinner. They had brought a few bushels of oysters and served them on the half shell and oyster stew with a generous supply of Lottie Dryden's crab cakes. Lottie was there to see that everything went just right. Needless to say, a few Budweiser longnecks were consumed that night. The affair was very special to everyone involved and would never be forgotten.

At around one thirty the next morning, Glenn Parrot was up in the wheel house getting a glass of water. He looked up at the boat shed and noticed a flash of light. He kept watching as two more flashes occurred. He yelled below.

"Get up! Everybody on deck! Someone's in the shed taking pictures!"

Even though most of the crew were still under the influence of the party, they tore out of their bunks, threw on their pants and raced to the shed. Inside, they found two men in bathing suits, each with a waterproof camera. They were quickly apprehended and led back to the *Queen* .

"I'll go call Sam, Glenn."

"Good idea, Jimmy."

The two intruders wouldn't say one word. No matter what the question or what was said to them, not a word came out of either one of them.

The fact that they had broken into the compound to look at the secret was undeniable. They had come in by water. Their scuba gear was discovered tied to the end of the dock.

Jimmy Firth returned after calling Sam. "Sam said to hold them aboard the *Queen* 'til morning and he'll be down first thing. He also said it was very important not to breath a word of this to anyone, not even the crew from Oxford. No wives, nobody!"

At eight thirty, Sam climbed aboard the *Queen*. The two intruders were in the wheel house with five of the *Muskrat* crew. As Sam entered, the rest of the boys and Allison appeared.

"Now, who do we have here?"

The two didn't even look at Sam, let alone answer him. They were two clean-cut caucasian males and both appeared to be in their mid-twenties.

"So you aren't going to talk to us, eh? Well now, what are we going to do with you?"

Sam thought for a minute. He motioned for Allison and whispered something in her ear. She responded in a whisper and dissappeared into her cabin. After about five minutes, she reappeared.

"Now, Bradley, I want you and Drake to accompany our guests to the forepeak, secure it, and come back here."

After doing so, Bradley and Drake joined the group in the wheel house.

Sam explained, "Those two guys, whoever they are, know the secret. We've got the cameras and film, but that's not enough. If we call the cops and turn these men over they'll spill the beans and the secret's out. We can't do that. If we do, whoever sent them will know the secret and know we're not changing it. We've got to hang onto them for a while."

"But that's kidnappin', Sam. We'll be arrested for kidnappin'. That's worse than what they did. They're only guilty of breakin' and enterin'. Kidnappin's a lot worse!"

"Maybe so Hoyt, but I'll take my chances. I want two or three men guarding them at all times. We might even anchor out so they can't get ashore."

"Oh that's a great idea, Sam. They'd never git ashore then." Bradley punched Drake in the ribs.

"Shut up, Drake. He already knows, you fool!"

After three days, the Perth Gazette newspaper reported that two of their employees were missing. The article explained that they had a wandered into the bush and had not returned. It was interesting that Brewer owned the newspaper.

Chapter Eleven

It had been the longest week ever, but it was finally over. Both boats were re-measured and put back in the water. The first race of the America's Cup was scheduled for one o'clock and the wind was blowing a steady twenty knots, gusting to twenty-three.

As the boats were being towed out, Hambden got a lump in his throat. The fact that they were in the America's Cup was finally sinking in.

The *Australia* was towing out right beside them and gave them a wave. Hoyt waved back and smiled. He noticed they were hobby-horsing quite a lot compared to the *Muskrat*. He was anxious to see just how much the Aussies had changed their boat.

The pre-race duties were performed aboard the *Muskrat* like clockwork in spite of all the butterflies.

Hoyt thought to himself, this is nothing special; it's just another race; do your job like you always do. It wasn't though, he was as nervous as a chickadee.

Hambden was too, and commented, "Hoyt, I'm a little nervous, how about you?"

"A little! I'm about to wet my pants. I've never been so scared."

Drake yelled up, "What the hell are you boys nervous about? We ain't got nothin' to loose. Shee-it! That Conners feller done took care of that!"

Australia III won the start, but *Muskrat* was only a half a boat length behind. Both boats carried their number two. It didn't take long to figure out that the Aussies had made radical changes in their boat. The *Australia* was not moving in the heavy air and large seas. The *Muskrat* beat her to the weather mark by nearly fifteen seconds. The margin widened on every leg except one when the *Muskrat* was very late getting her chute up. It was no contest. The *Muskrat* breezed to an easy win and was one up in the seven race series. Three wins to go and it was all over.

"Nick, I can't believe how easily we beat them. Can you?"

"It was a clean victory, Sam. The Aussies definitely have a brand new boat. They're gambling most of the races are going to be sailed in the lighter stuff. Don't you go and get real confident, Sam. Remember this time last year in the twelve meter worlds there was very little air. This is their home water. Don't forget that, Sam."

The next day they raced again and fortunately, for the *Muskrat*, it blew again. She won the race by over two minutes. Everything was going perfectly. The crew and the Eastern Shore contingency were beginning to relax. It seemed as though their problems were over. Only two races to go and the cup would be heading to Oxford, Maryland.

The weather forecast called for the heavy winds to continue and the Aussies called for a lay day, hoping for lighter winds. They guessed right and the third race was sailed in twelve to fifteen. As the race progressed, it was closer to twelve knots. The Aussies won by an incredible four minutes, eight seconds. The *Muskrat* syndicate was stunned. Everything had been going so well until now.

"It's up to Mother Nature, I'm afraid. We've made our

decision to stick with what we got."

"All we can do now is pray, Nick."

"Guess you're right, Sam, but we can call for a lay day. They're callin' for more light stuff tomorrow. I'd be tempted to ask for a day at the dock."

Sam contacted the committee and asked that no race be held the next day. The light airs were predominant the following day, but unfortunately for the Americans, it held for the day after and the Aussies tied the series, two to two. If it blew the *Muskrat* was the superior boat, but the Aussies had the advantage in anything less than fifteen. The Aussies gambled, and their gamble was looking like it may pay off.

The tables turned again in the fifth race of the series. The Doctor was back and with him came the *Muskrat* . She won by nearly thirty seconds.

Hambden and the crew felt much better, they had three victories under their belt and had two shots at the cup. The *Muskrat* was one up in the series going into race number six. "Give us one more day with the Doctor and it's all over." Hambden thought.

The press covered every jibe, set and tack. Never before in the history of the cup had the coverage been so complete. Sadly, however, the big story was the weather. Everyone was disappointed that it seemed to be the dominant factor.

As the boats approached the line for the sixth race, Sam was excited. The wind was up to twenty knots and building. It looked like a *Muskrat* day for sure.

As the race progressed, it seemed to prove Sam right, and as the boats rounded the weather mark and started the seventh leg, the *Muskrat* had a commanding lead. It was just a matter of time before Hoyt, Hambden, and the *Muskrat* crew would get the gun and take home all the marbles.

The spinnaker set was a little slow after they rounded the mark, but Hambden didn't care. Their lead was a good one.

"Just don't make any mistakes on this jibe gang. This should be the last one for the series. We'll drink beer tomorrow."

"Bull shit! We'll drink beer today." Drake grabbed a longneck. The *Muskrat* was probably the first boat to sail the America's Cup while her crew was downing a few longnecks.

"Okay, trim, Allison!" They were jibing.

The wind was picking up and the seas were building. As the main came around, they surfed off a huge wave.

The boom got somewhat out of control and quickly flopped to the starboard side. It happened more quickly than usual. They rounded the leeward mark a comfortable forty five seconds ahead.

"All right, gang, this is it! Just git this son-of-a-bitch to the finish line and we're heros. The cup is ours!" Hambden was hyped.

"Drive her ,Hoyt!" Drake yelled from below.

"Vaughn, git your ass in that cockpit boy! You git overboard now, ain't nobody pickin' you up!" Schuyler was feeling great and giving Vaughn a little grief.

Sam and the group back aboard the *Queen* went crazy. "Get ready with the champagne. It'll be over soon." Sam was like a little kid on a Christmas morning.

All of a sudden Nick's jaw dropped. Sam saw his expression and as he looked back at the *Muskrat* , witnessed the heartbreaking sight of her mast falling into the water. No one said a word for nearly ten seconds. The cup was so close yet now so far away. The *Muskrat* crew felt as if they had been robbed, as the *Australia* sailed by and got the gun. The series was tied at three all.

"What could have happened, Nick?"

"Sam, remember the last jibe? There was no running backstay on and maybe that's what weakened the spar. I'm not sure."

"I am sure of one thing. If we loose our spar the next race, we'll loose the cup. There's only one more."

Sam requested a lay day and a new mast was installed. Nick seemed to be satisfied with it.

At eleven o'clock, they untied the *Muskrat* and hooked up to the *Oxford Queen* . Unfortunately for the *Muskrat*, the wind was light, blowing less than twelve. It seemed so unfair that after such an all out effort, the weather on one day would determine the outcome. The entire crew was down. The wind was blowing less than twelve. A front had been predicted, but not until the evening. Eight to twelve knots were predicted for the race.

Nick was very disappointed. He had worked so hard on the design, figuring she would be sailing in heavy wind. He had nothing to be ashamed of. His boat was on its way out for the final race of the America's Cup. Only two designers could boast that on this day, and he was one of them. Nick still questioned his decision not to change her during the last week, however.

Even though it seemed impossible, the spectator fleet had grown in number. Maybe there were more smaller boats because of the lack of winds. It was an awesome sight. People lined the shore. Several boats displayed large banners. One of the larger ones read "You Can't Pack With The *Rat* ."

No one on the crew said a word. It was as if they were being led by the *Queen* to slaughter. The stakes were higher than ever before and their chances of winning were just the opposite.

"Listen, you all." Drake Cochran got everyone's attention.

"I ain't the fanciest sailor on this boat. I'm just here to row that machine down there, but there ain't nobody on here wants to win this race no more than me. Now you all act like we've already made her over into the marine hearse we was talkin' about. We ain't lost yet! Shee-it, the race ain't even started. We ain't lost, and I ain't givin' up neither. Nobody's givin' up! There are people all over the world rootin' for us out here. We're racin' today for all the little guys, all the guys that's been told they can't win. The *Muskrat's* been the underdog the whole way, but we ain't never gived up." Drake was very emotional as a tear came to his eye. "Well, ain't no way we're gonna give up now. We can't let 'em down. Let's give it our best shot, damn it! We can do it! I know we can!" Every inch of Drake was committed to winning the cup. Sir Thomas Lipton, with his unforgettable obsession to take the cup to England, didn't want it any more than Drake.

His comments seemed to brighten the crew's spirits. "He's right, Hoyt. Hell, anything can happen today."

"We'll do our damn best, Hambden. That's all anybody can ask."

They hoisted the light number one and had the heavy number one to starboard and the number two in the port locker.

At the five minute gun, the two boats began to maneuver for the best start. With two minutes to go, it was the dog chasing its tail routine, both boats following each other in a tight circle. With twenty seconds to go, *Australia* broke off and went for the line.

"Not yet, Hoyt. Not yet!" The *Muskrat* held off for a few seconds. "Now! Go! Go for it!"

The *Muskrat* was one boat length directly behind the *Australia* , both boats on starboard tack.

"She's gonna be early Hoyt; we're fine. Drive this bitch!"

The gun fired and *Australia* was called over. She had to go back in the light air. *Muskrat* passed her and headed upwind toward the first mark. By the time *Australia* had returned to the line and re-started, she was over a minute and a half behind. It was a very costly error. As the boats worked to weather, *Australia* gained, but not much. The *Muskrat* held a minute fifteen second lead at the mark.

On the downwind leg, the huge main of the *Muskrat* paid off and she nearly held off the Aussies completely, giving up only six seconds. The second weather leg was a costly one for the American boat. The wind dropped to less than ten knots and the Aussies were closing the gap fast.

Hambden kept looking for signs of fresh air on the water with his binoculars. "I think I see some air ahead, Hoyt. There are ripples on the water up there. That's fresh air. Thank God!"

The *Australia* tacked for the sixth time of the leg. "I'm gonna gamble, Hoyt. Don't cover her. Let's go for the air ahead. The *Muskrat* continued on port tack and went far to the right of the course, seeking more of a breeze. *Australia* went over to starboard, staying more in the middle of the race course. Everybody held their breath.

"If we git a break now, we could git one hell of a lead, Sam."

"I don't like it, Nick. It's too early in the race for such a gamble."

That wasn't the case in Hambden's way of thinking. He figured they were definitely the slower boat in the light air, and now was the only time he would have a chance to gamble. Once *Australia* took the lead, she'd cover the *Muskrat* like a wet blanket. It had to be now or never.

The *Muskrat* sailed into more air. It increased from eight to eleven knots and she accelerated a little. "That's what we need, Hoyt. Keep her movin' boy. *Australia* doesn't have it yet.

You're movin' on her."

The wind lifted the *Muskrat*. "We don't want a lift now. We need a header so we can tack and make the mark on port."

Within a few seconds, *Australia* had gotten into the fresh air. She got headed badly, so she tacked and was laying the mark.

The *Muskrat* had lost the gamble; they had found the air first, but they were on the wrong side of the course when it changed direction. *Australia* rounded the weather mark thirty-two seconds ahead; the *Muskrat* had lost the lead. *Australia* picked up another eight seconds on the two reaching legs rounding the leeward mark forty seconds ahead. Things looked grim for the American boat.

Hambden continued to look for more air. "Maybe that cloud will bring a breeze," he thought. There was a very dark bank of clouds hanging over Rottnest Island dead to weather.

As they beat toward the mark, they were on the sixth leg of the race, leaving only one more run and then the final beat to weather. The America's Cup was almost over.

Australia rounded the mark forty-three seconds ahead. Her spinnaker set was perfect. When the *Muskrat* rounded the mark the wind seemed to pick up. Hambden looked aft and saw the dark cloud getting closer. The sky had turned pitch black over Rottnest Island; a squall was making up.

Hambden thought to himself, "It's our only chance."

He yelled to Schuyler, "Sky, put the number three on the headstay ready to go. Put the light number one below."

Schuyler didn't understand until he looked aft and saw the squall building. "Good call, Hambden."

As they got closer to the downwind mark, the wind started increasing, enabling them to close slightly on *Australia*. All of a sudden, there was a blinding bolt of lightning accompanied immediately with a loud clap of thunder, the storm hit and it was blowing forty knots before anyone knew it.

Pow! The spinnaker blew, ripping its seam down the middle.

"Get the number three up! Forget the chute. Make sure there are no knots in the sheets and guys."

They rounded the leeward mark as the rain came down in buckets. The spinnaker was in shreads, trailing behind the boat.

"That chute is killin' us flappin' back there. Let everything go, both sheets and the halyard. Let 'em go!"

The halyard and the sheets were released and the spinnaker slowly floated down into the ocean, no longer attached to the *Muskrat* .

"Ease the main, Allison. Let it flop. I can't handle it now."

The *Muskrat* was moving well in the breeze. Visibility was zero. Hoyt couldn't see the bow of the boat from the helm. The rain was hitting him in the face so hard he could barely keep his eyes open. No one had had time to put their foul weather gear on and it was cold.

"Let me have my hat." Hoyt needed the brim to catch the driving rain so he could see.

"We're headed slightly, Hoyt. Ready about!" Hambden ordered a tack.

The *Muskrat* pounded as she went head to wind in the forty knot winds.

"How are we doin', Hambden?"

"Hoyt, I have no idea where *Australia* is, but the loran says we're 'bout half way up the weather leg and the mark bears one hundred and ninety-five degrees. Thank God for these instruments!"

Just as Hambden said that, a bolt of lightning hit the spar of the *Muskrat* , shorting out every instrument aboard the boat.

"Oh shee-it! We've lost our loran!"

Seconds later, a fifty knot gust of wind hit. The *Muskrat* took a big knock down, putting the eased boom in the water. Hoyt lost his steerage and the boat began to broach.

"Hang on! She's broaching!" Hoyt yelled to the crew. Lightning and thunder were everywhere.

Hambden heard a loud crack. He was surprised it wasn't accompanied by a lightning bolt. Then he noticed what it was; the boom had broken.

"The boom's gone! It broke! Git the spinnaker pole back here, Sky. Hurry up before we break it all the way."

The boom was broken in the middle at about a one hundred and sixty degree angle. The crew managed to lash the pole on the boom and prevented any further bending.

"Should we tack, Hambden?"

"I don't know, Hoyt. I don't know where the damn finish line is." Visibility was still zero and Hambden had been working on the boom, not being able to concentrate on where they were on the course.

"We'd better go. I guess we're not far from the finish line. Everybody keep your eyes open. Let's tack!"

Hoyt rolled the boat over to starboard tack. The boys below worked their hearts out.

"I'm glad I ain't on one'a them can boats, Bradley."

"What do ya mean can boats, Drake?"

"Them metal boats. Ain't that Aussie boat metal?"

"You talkin' about the lightnin'?"

"Yeah. I'm glad I ain't on her."

The *Muskrat* was hanging on well with her broken boom. Hambden wished he knew where the *Australia* had gone in the storm. Visibility was still zero and they had no idea whether or not they were catching *Australia* . The rains continued to come down hard, but the winds began to subside.

"Let's go to the number two, boys!"

Within twenty seconds, the new sail was up.

"At least we haven't heard a gun, Hambden. The Aussies haven't finished yet."

"By God you're right!. I never thought about that, Hoyt. We gotta be close to the line too." In less than five seconds, their hopes were dashed by a loud "Bang".

"Oh no! That was the gun! They've finished! We've lost!"

Nobody said a word. Even though they were very close to the finish line, it just wasn't to be. They had sailed a tough race, but there had been too much light air. It was all over. As Hambden turned and looked at Hoyt's expression, he realized that it was all over. Hoyt's dream, the dream of the entire crew of the *Muskrat* was no more. The hopes of all of Oxford and countless thousands from around the world were dashed. The *Muskrat* and her crew had made a valiant effort, but had come up one race short. Despite overcoming almost insurmountable odds, the *Muskrat* had lost the cup.

The visibility was still poor, but had improved slightly. It seemed that the spectator fleet had wandered onto the race course and Hambden was annoyed. "Gawd damn spectator fleet's all around us. Shee-it, there's the *Queen* comin' right at us and we're still racin'. Can't we at least finish the race with some gawd damn respect?"

Just then Allison Deemer screamed as she pointed behind the boat. "There's the mark! I see the mark! It's behind us! See it? It's behind us! I can't believe it!"

"Behind us! You see the mark behind us? Where?" As Hambden looked aft, he saw the mark and behind it another twelve meter.

The mark they saw was the mark of the finish line, and the

twelve they saw behind was *Australia.*

"Gawd damn, we're over, we've finished, we won! The gun was for us! We won! We won! We've won the America's Cup!"

The *Muskrat* had crossed the finish line without realizing it. As the pouring rain turned into a slow drizzle, they saw *Australia* cross the line. The *Muskrat* had passed her in the storm. The *Rat* had captured the cup.

It was finally over. There would be no more tacks, no more jibes, no more sailing. The America's Cup was on its way to a sleepy little town in the United States on the Eastern Shore of Maryland. The group from Oxford had captured the most prized trophy in yachting. They had won the America's Cup.

The tow back to Fishing Boat Harbor was more moving than anything that had taken place before. It was indescribable. The numbers of boats and people were incredible. The horns, whistles, sirens and bells were deafening. The *Muskrat* had been the underdog since October, and soon after she was everyone's favorite. People from every country, even *Australia,* were pulling for her. Surrounding the *Muskrat,* hundreds of American flags flew proudly in the breeze. *Muskrat's* followers were in a frenzy. Schuyler turned back to see if Hoyt was crying. There in the cockpit were Hoyt, Hambden, Allison and Drake with their arms around each other, everyone with tears running down their cheeks.

Later that day there was a presentation of the cup to Sam and the *Muskrat* crew. It was held at the *Muskrat* compound. The many Americans that attended were very proud, especially those from Maryland's Eastern Shore. The ceremony was very nice. It was also very simple and brief. Sam noticed the two reporters that were lost in the bush were in the audience.

The Commodore of the Royal Perth Yacht Club made a short statement before handing the Cup to Samuel E. Johnson,

III. "Sir, this must be a very special day for you. I know you're very proud of the *Muskrat* and its crew. I have been privileged to have watched every race in which you sailed. I have never observed a more dedicated and hard working bunch of men and women in my life. No matter what the odds, no matter what the conditions, no matter what; they never gave up. When you arrived in Perth in September, not only did no one give you a chance of winning, most thought you were in, as you say, "over your heads". Well, you have taught all of us what you Eastern Shoremen are all about. It gives me great pleasure to present to you the America's Cup."

The crowd exploded, as did several bottles of champagne as the corks were popped.

Sam and Hoyt together held the cup above their heads. Hoyt began to cry. In the middle of the tremendous celebration, someone passed a telephone receiver toward Sam.

"The President of the United States would like a word with you, sir. "

Drake had quaffed a few beers by this time and grabbed the phone. He spoke into the receiver, "Shee-it! This ain't the gawd damn president. Who the hell is this?"

Hoyt quickly took the phone. "Shut up, Drake!"

The President congratulated Sam and said he was very proud of the "Oxford Crew." "This is a proud day for the United States. It is another example of our ingenuity and our relentless pursuit for excellence. The entire nation should be very proud."

After a few comments, Sam passed the phone back.

A number of people in the crowd started chanting, "What's the secret? What's the secret?"

Sam motioned Nick Benson to the podium. "Ladies and gentlemen, I know you have been waiting a long time to find

Muskrat

out what the *Muskrat's* secret is. Well, the secret goes back in my family three generations. My granddaddy, Ralph Benson, came up with it. I sure wish he was here today. He would be very proud. He was kinda like the *Muskrat*; granddaddy had a little something that all them other builders didn't have. He was special. Well, you're about to see his secret." He gave the signal for the crane to lift the twelve out of the water. Everyone speculated about what the keel looked like.

"I'll bet there's a bulb on the bottom of it."

"I think it's a wing with a trim tab," said another. "I think there's a rudder on the keel," was a third explanation.

As the *Muskrat* came out of the water, the crowd experienced the surprise of their lives. To everyone's amazement there was no keel at all. Nick Benson looked at the thousands of people and smiled as the crowd started buzzing. They were absolutely astounded.

Several questions were heard: "What keeps her on her feet? How does she keep from side-slipping on the wind?"

Nick motioned to Glenn Parrot who went below. The *Muskrat's* bow was pointing toward the people. Out of the bottom of the boat slowly emerged a very large and unusual centerboard. It was, however, not at the very bottom of the hull, but instead protruded about a third of the way up from the bottom's center toward the waterline. It came out on a forty-five degree angle. This furthur confused everyone. As they continued to watch, a second centerboard appeared on the other side; again about one third from the center at a forty-five degree angle.

Nick's secret was ingenious. He had installed no keel but instead placed two centerboards in the hull. When the *Muskrat* was on starboard tack, the port board was lowered and the starboard board brought up flush with the hull. The boards were extremely heavy so the board that was up on the weather side gave a tremendous righting effect to the boat. The board that was down was directly under the boat because of the heel, and the leading edge was cocked toward the center line. This automatically lifted the boat to weather. Nick's secret was truly a breakthrough. It made the Australian's wing keel look as though it was developed in the stone age.

Nick explained the theory to everyone and asked if there were any questions. He had already explained to the crew about how the old skipjack, *Maggie P.'s* board worked. It was the same shape, but she had only one. The secret was simple. She was always climbing to weather because the board was also cocked to weather. The aft end of the centerboard well was oversized in width. When the boat heeled, the aft end of the board would slide down, thus creating a lifting effect.

At first, the explanation seemed confusing, but soon it was as simple as night and day.

"Mr. Benson, the first two races for the *Muskrat* were very slow and as a result, you were called upon to find out why. What was the problem?"

"It was very simple. You remember that the boat was only slow off the wind and only on the port tack. I discovered that the port centerboard was jamming and couldn't be raised all the way up. On port tack, the starboard centerboard was, of course, at least partially down. By having both boards down, each pointing toward the bow, they acted like a brake, like a snow plow. That's why the boat stopped.

"On the other hand, when she jibed over to starboard, the port board was supposed to be down and the other one was raised. She regained her speed then."

It seemed so simple, once explained by the old master, but it would change yachting design for years to come.

"Mr. Benson, it's hard to believe that your centerboards are heavy enough to keep a twelve meter on her feet in heavy winds. Obviously, they do, but could you tell us what there made of?"

"Sir, I've explained the rowin' machines, the boat's layout and the ruddynut. By the way, Mr. Johnson and I have started a little business, if anybody's interested in buying some of that wood. I've explained the centerboards, too; but I ain't tellin' ya 'bout what them boards is made of. We can't tell all our secrets. Who knows? Maybe us boys from Oxford might have to go bring this cup back home again."